This

ONE-MINUTE POCKET BIBLE

Presented To

_____

_____

By

_____

_____

Date

_____

ONE-MINUTE POCKET BIBLE

BY MIKE MURDOCK

*Wisdom is the principal thing; therefore get
wisdom: and with all thy getting get understanding.*
Proverbs 4:7

Wisdom International
P.O. Box 747
Dallas, Texas
75221

Unless otherwise indicated, all Scripture quotations are taken from the *King James Version* of the Bible.

One-Minute Pocket Bible For The Achiever
ISBN 1-56394-020-5
Copyright © 1994 by Mike Murdock
P.O. Box 99
Dallas, Texas 75221

Published By
Wisdom International
P.O. Box 747
Dallas, Texas 75221

TABLE OF CONTENTS

TABLE OF CONTENTS

TABLE OF CONTENTS

FACTS ABOUT ACHIEVERS

Achievers come from every walk of life. There are no barriers due to economic status, race, religion or even age. Anyone can be an achiever. Achievers have both low and high IQs. There has been some negative talk that achievers are driven and that they put too much pressure on themselves to succeed. As with anything, I'm sure there are some who go overboard. Still, the achiever possesses characteristics that everyone should desire.

In simple terms, achievers are motivated to act and accomplish. They aren't afraid to dream and then take the initiative and act upon it. They are productive with their time. They set goals and work to achieve those goals.

Achievers have a sense of purpose. It's not that they don't face obstacles, because they do. Yet they strive to overcome their obstacles. They have an intelligent plan of action that includes being realistic about their strengths and weaknesses.

What sets achievers apart from others is their ability to "see down the road." Because they have a goal in mind, they are not moved or hindered by momentary stumbling blocks or setbacks.

The Bible is a book full of stories about achievers. Joseph was an achiever. The book of Genesis, starting in chapter 37, relays his story. This dreamer faced horrendous obstacles, but was a winner in the end.

The book of Nehemiah is worthy of examination regarding achievers. This short book of only 11 chapters chronicles the story of the long and slow process of the rebuilding of Jerusalem by a people who were steadfast in their mission. Again, they faced many problems, but they overcame their difficulties by the help of God.

Jesus was an achiever. The early prophecies and later record of His life is full of the attributes of an achiever. Isaiah 50:7 prophesies of His determination and confidence. "For the Lord GOD will help me; therefore shall I not be confounded: therefore have I set my face like a flint, and I know that I shall not be ashamed."

Hebrews 12:2 states, "Looking unto Jesus the author and finisher of [our] faith; who for the joy that was set before him endured the cross, despising the shame, and is set down at the right hand of the throne of God." Jesus had a goal and endured even a shameful death because of the "joy that was set before Him." He could see beyond the moment.

Paul and Timothy were achievers. Philippians 1:6 states, "Being confident of this very thing, that he which hath begun a good work in you will perform [it] until the day of Jesus Christ." Above all, achievers are confident.

Interestingly, two Greek words for "faith" denote traits of the achiever. The word "elpis" in the Greek means "to anticipate with pleasure," "expectation," and "confidence." The Greek word "peitho" means "confident." Achievers are men and women of faith and vision.

That being the case, the entire chapter of Hebrews 11 heralds the great achievers in Biblical history. Some 40 verses detail the insight, determination, strengths, obstacles and victories of these great men and women of Biblical history.

But is the achiever a product of inherent behavior? If this is the case, your spiritual heritage is unequaled. You are an achiever by rightful inheritance. More probably, however, the achiever possesses his nature by learned behavior. For example, a child takes his first steps. The parents clap with glee and encourage him to continue. Understandably, the thrill of victory motivates him to continue. When he falls, he is helped back up and coaxed to try again. He is encouraged and usually rewarded. Through this positive process, he learns to become an achiever.

Life is full of ups and downs, but the achiever sees these challenges as invitations to greatness. Perhaps it's all in how you see the whole picture. The achiever sees the glass half full while others sees it half empty.

As an achiever you can be proud of the attributes you enjoy. Strive to channel your energies in positive, productive efforts. Learn to live Matthew 6:33, which states, "But seek ye first the kingdom of God, and his right-eousness; and all these things shall be added unto you."

AN ACHIEVER'S PRAYER

Good Morning Heavenly Father!

I am very busy today, but knew I needed to stop and talk to you before rushing into my day.

Forgive me for being too aggressive at times and rushing into projects that I never brought to you in prayer. I've done so many stupid things and made some wrong decisions, yet you have kept your hand upon me. I'm so thankful for that.

Now purge my agenda today. Take out of my life those who break my focus off your assignments. Bring into my life those who grow your dream within me.

Protect me. Talk to me. Keep your angels around me every hour of this day.

I will speak your name with joy and thanksgiving. I will celebrate your presence and tell others of your laws.

I shall embrace your wisdom every single day of my life.

In Jesus Name,

Amen

THE
ACHIEVER'S
ONE-MINUTE
POCKET BIBLE

ABILITIES

For the LORD shall be thy confidence,
Proverbs 3:26a

Not by might, nor by power, but by my spirit, saith the LORD of hosts.   *Zechariah 4:6b*

Verily, verily, I say unto you, He that believeth on me, the works that I do shall he do also; and greater works than these shall he do; because I go unto my Father.   *John 14:12*

What shall we then say to these things? If God be for us, who can be against us?   *Romans 8:31*

But we have the mind of Christ.
I Corinthians 2:16b

And let us not be weary in well doing: for in due season we shall reap, if we faint not.
Galatians 6:9

I can do all things through Christ which strengtheneth me.   *Philippians 4:13*

For the gifts and calling of God are without repentance.   *Romans 11:29*

NOTHING IS EVER AS DIFFICULT AS IT FIRST APPEARS.

1

ACHIEVEMENT

Lord, all my desire is before thee;

Psalms 38:9a

The soul of the sluggard desireth, and hath nothing: but the soul of the diligent shall be made fat.

Proverbs 13:4

So shall my word be that goeth forth out of my mouth: it shall not return unto me void, but it shall accomplish that which I please, and it shall prosper in the thing whereto I sent it.   *Isaiah 55:11*

The LORD is good unto them that wait for him, to the soul that seeketh him.   *Lamentations 3:25*

Therefore I say unto you, What things soever ye desire, when ye pray, believe that ye receive them, and ye shall have them.   *Mark 11:24*

But without faith it is impossible to please him: for he that cometh to God must believe that he is, and that he is a rewarder of them that diligently seek him.   *Hebrews 11:6*

EVERY CREATION CONTAINS AN INVISIBLE COMMAND FROM GOD TO MULTIPLY AND BECOME MORE.

APPEARANCE

But the LORD said unto Samuel, Look not on his countenance, or on the height of his stature; because I have refused him: for the LORD seeth not as man seeth; for man looketh on the outward appearance, but the LORD looketh on the heart.

I Samuel 16:7

For the LORD taketh pleasure in his people: he will beautify the meek with salvation.

Psalms 149:4

A merry heart maketh a cheerful countenance: but by sorrow of the heart the spirit is broken.

Proverbs 15:13

Do ye look on things after the outward appearance? If any man trust to himself that he is Christ's, let him of himself think this again, that, as he is Christ's, even so are we Christ's.

II Corinthians 10:7

Whose adorning let it not be that outward adorning of plaiting the hair, and of wearing of gold, or of putting on of apparel; But let it be the hidden man of the heart, in that which is not corruptible, even the ornament of a meek and quiet spirit, which is in the sight of God of great price. I Peter 3:3-4

PEOPLE SEE WHAT YOU ARE BEFORE THEY HEAR WHAT YOU ARE.

ASSIGNMENT

Let every man abide in the same calling wherein he was called.   *I Corinthians 7:20*

And let the beauty of the LORD our God be upon us: and establish thou the work of our hands upon us; yea, the work of our hands establish thou it.
Psalms 90:17

And thine ears shall hear a word behind thee, saying, This is the way, walk ye in it, when ye turn to the right hand, and when ye turn to the left.
Isaiah 30:21

Seest thou a man diligent in his business? He shall stand before kings; he shall not stand before mean men.   *Proverbs 22:29*

For promotion cometh neither from the east, nor from the west, nor from the south. But God is the judge: he putteth down one, and setteth up another.
Psalms 75:6-7

YOUR ASSIGNMENT IS DECIDED BY GOD AND DISCOVERED BY YOU. IT IS GEOGRAPHICAL AND IS ALWAYS TO A PERSON OR PEOPLE. IT IS ALWAYS TO SOLVE A PROBLEM FOR SOMEONE.

ATTITUDE

Teach me, and I will hold my tongue: and cause me to understand wherein I have erred.   *Job 6:24*

For out of the abundance of the heart the mouth speaketh. But I say unto you, That every idle word that men shall speak, they shall give account thereof in the day of judgment. For by thy words thou shalt be justified, and by thy words thou shalt be condemned.   *Matthew 12:34b, 36-37*

Be ye angry, and sin not: let not the sun go down upon your wrath: *Ephesians 4:26*

Grudge not one against another, brethren, lest ye be condemned: behold, the judge standeth before the door.   *James 5:9*

Let your conversation be without covetousness; and be content with such things as ye have: for he hath said, I will never leave thee, nor forsake thee.
     Hebrews 13:5

YOUR ATTITUDE DETERMINES THE SEASONS YOU ENTER.

BIBLE

Ye shall not add unto the word which I command you, neither shall ye diminish ought from it, that ye may keep the commandments of the LORD your God which I command you.   *Deuteronomy 4:2*

The law of the LORD is perfect, converting the soul: the testimony of the LORD is sure, making wise the simple.   *Psalms 19:7*

Thy word have I hid in mine heart, that I might not sin against thee. Thy word is a lamp unto my feet, and a light unto my path.   *Psalms 119:11, 105*

Heaven and earth shall pass away: but my words shall not pass away.   *Mark 13:31*

All scripture is given by inspiration of God, and is profitable for doctrine, for reproof, for correction, for instruction in righteousness: That the man of God may be perfect, thoroughly furnished unto all good works.   *II Timothy 3:16, 17*

For the word of God is quick, and powerful, and sharper than any twoedged sword, piercing even to the dividing asunder of soul and spirit, and of the joints and marrow, and is a discerner of the thoughts and intents of the heart.   *Hebrews 4:12*

GOD'S ONLY NEED IS TO BE BELIEVED. HIS ONLY PAIN IS TO BE DOUBTED.

BUSINESS

Go to the ant, thou sluggard; consider her ways, and be wise: Which having no guide, overseer, or ruler, Provideth her meat in the summer, and gathereth her food in the harvest.   *Proverbs 6:6-8*

Seest thou a man diligent in his business? he shall stand before kings; he shall not stand before mean men.   *Proverbs 22:29*

He that tilleth his land shall have plenty of bread: but he that followeth after vain persons shall have poverty enough.   *Proverbs 28:19*

When I applied mine heart to know wisdom, and to see the business that is done upon the earth: for also there is that neither day nor night seeth sleep with his eyes: *Ecclesiastes 8:16*

Not slothful in business; fervent in spirit; serving the Lord; Rejoicing in hope; patient in tribulation; continuing instant in prayer;   *Romans 12:12*

And that ye study to be quiet, and to do your own business, and to work with your own hands, as we commanded you;   *I Thessalonians 4:11*

IF GOD IS YOUR PARTNER YOU CAN AFFORD TO MAKE BIG PLANS.

CHARACTER

Blessed is the man that walketh not in the counsel of the ungodly, nor standeth in the way of sinners, nor sitteth in the seat of the scornful. But his delight is in the law of the LORD; and in his law doth he meditate day and night. *Psalms 1:1-2*

Judge me, O LORD; for I have walked in mine integrity: I have trusted also in the LORD; therefore I shall not slide. *Psalms 26:1*

And as for me, thou upholdest me in mine integrity, and settest me before thy face for ever.
Psalms 41:12

Recompense to no man evil for evil. Provide things honest in the sight of all men. If it be possible, as much as lieth in you, live peaceably with all men.
Romans 12:17-18

Finally, brethren, whatsoever things are true, whatsoever things are honest, whatsoever things are just, whatsoever things are pure, whatsoever things are lovely, whatsoever things are of good report; if there be any virtue, and if there be any praise, think on these things. *Philippians 4:8*

Let integrity and uprightness preserve me; for I wait on thee. *Psalms 25:21*

YOU CANNOT BE WHAT YOU'RE NOT, BUT YOU CAN BECOME WHAT YOU'RE NOT.

CHURCH ATTENDANCE

And let them make me a sanctuary; that I may
dwell among them. *Exodus 25:8*

One thing have I desired of the LORD, that will I
seek after; that I may dwell in the house of the
LORD all the days of my life, to behold the beauty
of the LORD, and to inquire in his temple.
Psalms 27:4

I was glad when they said unto me, Let us go into
the house of the LORD. *Psalms 122:1*

Keep thy foot when thou goest to the house of
God, and be more ready to hear, than to give the sac-
rifice of fools: for they consider not that they do evil.
Ecclesiastes 5:1

For where two or three are gathered together in
my name, there am I in the midst of them.
Matthew 18:20

Not forsaking the assembling of ourselves
together, as the manner of some is; but exhorting
one another: and so much the more, as ye see the
day approaching. *Hebrews 10:25*

**CLIMATE DETERMINES WHAT GROWS
WITHIN YOU.**

COMMITMENT

Commit thy way unto the LORD; trust also in
him; and he shall bring it to pass.   *Psalms 37:5*

Commit thy works unto the LORD, and thy
thoughts shall be established.   *Proverbs 16:3*

He staggered not at the promise of God through
unbelief; but was strong in faith, giving glory to
God; And being fully persuaded that, what he had
promised, he was able also to perform.
Romans 4:20-21

And let us not be weary in well doing: for in due
season we shall reap, if we faint not.
Galatians 6:9

Brethren, I count not myself to have apprehended:
but this one thing I do, forgetting those things which
are behind, and reaching forth unto those things
which are before, I press toward the mark for the
prize of the high calling of God in Christ Jesus.
Philippians 3:13-14

**COMMITMENT IS YOUR FINAL DECISION TO
MEET THE NEEDS OF THE ONES GOD'S CALLED
YOU TO SERVICE.**

COMMUNICATION

And thine ears shall hear a word behind thee, saying, This is the way, walk ye in it, when ye turn to the right hand, and when ye turn to the left.
Isaiah 30:21

Be not deceived: evil communications corrupt good manners. *I Corinthians 15:33*

Let him that is taught in the word communicate unto him that teacheth in all good things.
Galatians 6:6

Let no corrupt communication proceed out of your mouth, but that which is good to the use of edifying, that it may minister grace unto the hearers.
Ephesians 4:29

Notwithstanding ye have well done, that ye did communicate with my affliction.
Philippians 4:14

But now ye also put off all these; anger, wrath, malice, blasphemy, filthy communication out of your mouth. *Colossians 3:8*

IF WHAT YOU SAY TO SOMEONE CANNOT BE SAID TO EVERYONE, THEN SAY IT TO NO ONE!
J. E. MURDOCK

COMPASSION

But he, being full of compassion, forgave their iniquity, and destroyed them not: yea, many a time turned he his anger away, and did not stir up all his wrath.   *Psalms 78:38*

Unto the upright there ariseth light in the darkness: he is gracious, and full of compassion, and righteous.   *Psalms 112:4*

Can a woman forget her sucking child, that she should not have compassion on the son of her womb? Yea, they may forget, yet will I not forget thee.   *Isaiah 49:15*

And Jesus, when he came out, saw much people, and was moved with compassion toward them, because they were as sheep not having a shepherd: and he began to teach them many things.
                                           Mark 6:34

Finally, be ye all of one mind, having compassion one of another, love as brethren, be pitiful, be courteous: *I Peter 3:8*

THOSE WHO UNLOCK YOUR COMPASSION ARE THOSE TO WHOM YOU HAVE BEEN ASSIGNED.

COURAGE

Be strong and of a good courage, fear not, nor be afraid of them: for the LORD thy God, he it is that doth go with thee; he will not fail thee, nor forsake thee.   *Deuteronomy 31:6*

Have not I commanded thee? Be strong and of a good courage; be not afraid, neither be thou dismayed: for the LORD thy God is with thee whithersoever thou goest.   *Joshua 1:9*

Be of good courage, and he shall strengthen your heart, all ye that hope in the LORD.
Psalms 31:24

There shall no evil befall thee, neither shall any plague come nigh thy dwelling.   *Psalms 91:10*

Strengthen ye the weak hands, and confirm the feeble knees.   *Isaiah 35:3*

Fear thou not; for I am with thee: be not dismayed; for I am thy God: I will strengthen thee; yea, I will help thee; yea, I will uphold thee with the right hand of my righteousness.   *Isaiah 41:10*

I can do all things through Christ which strengtheneth me.   *Philippians 4:13*

WINNERS ARE JUST EX-LOSERS WHO GOT MAD.

CRISIS

Yea, though I walk through the valley of the shadow of death, I will fear no evil: for thou art with me; thy rod and thy staff they comfort me.

Psalms 23:4

For in the time of trouble he shall hide me in his pavilion: in the secret of his tabernacle shall he hide me; he shall set me up upon a rock.   *Psalms 27:5*

My soul shall make her boast in the LORD: the humble shall hear thereof, and be glad. O magnify the LORD with me, and let us exalt his name together. I sought the LORD, and he heard me, and delivered me from all my fears.

Psalms 34:2-4

God is our refuge and strength, a very present help in trouble. Therefore will not we fear, though the earth be removed, and though the mountains be carried into the midst of the sea; Though the waters thereof roar and be troubled, though the mountains shake with the swelling thereof.

Psalms 46:1-3

I will not leave you comfortless: I will come to you.   *John 14:18*

CRISIS ALWAYS OCCURS AT THE CURVE OF CHANGE.

CRITICISM

A soft answer turneth away wrath: but grievous words stir up anger.   *Proverbs 15:1*

Blessed are ye, when men shall revile you, and persecute you, and shall say all manner of evil against you falsely, for my sake.   *Matthew 5:11*

But I say unto you, Love your enemies, bless them that curse you, do good to them that hate you, and pray for them which despitefully use you, and persecute you;   *Matthew 5:44*

And the soldiers likewise demanded of him, saying, And what shall we do? And he said unto them, Do violence to no man, neither accuse any falsely; and be content with your wages.   *Luke 3:14*

But love ye your enemies, and do good, and lend, hoping for nothing again; and your reward shall be great, and ye shall be the children of the Highest: for he is kind unto the unthankful and to the evil.
      Luke 6:35

Having a good conscience; that, whereas they speak evil of you, as of evildoers, they may be ashamed that falsely accuse your good conversation in Christ.   *1 Peter 3:16*

NEVER SPEND MORE TIME ON A CRITIC THAN YOU WOULD GIVE TO A FRIEND.

DEBT

The wicked borroweth, and payeth not again: but the righteous showeth mercy, and giveth.

Psalms 37:21

He that is surety for a stranger shall smart for it: and he that hateth suretiship is sure.

Proverbs 11:15

The rich ruleth over the poor, and the borrower is servant to the lender.

Proverbs 22:7

Give, and it shall be given unto you; good measure, pressed down, and shaken together, and running over, shall men give into your bosom. For with the same measure that ye mete withal it shall be measured to you again.

Luke 6:38

Owe no man any thing, but to love one another:

Romans 13:8a

Beloved, I wish above all things that thou mayest prosper and be in health, even as thy soul prospereth.

III John 1:2

Thou shalt not borrow.

Deuteronomy 28:12b

DEBT IS PROOF OF GREED. IT IS THE OPPOSITE OF GIVING. DEBT IS EMPTYING YOUR FUTURE TO FILL UP YOUR PRESENT. GIVING IS EMPTYING YOUR PRESENT TO FILL UP YOUR FUTURE.

DECISION MAKING

And if it seem evil unto you to serve the LORD, choose you this day whom ye will serve; whether the gods which your fathers served that were on the other side of the flood, or the gods of the Amorites, in whose land ye dwell: but as for me and my house, we will serve the LORD.   *Joshua 24:15*

Trust in the LORD with all thine heart; and lean not unto thine own understanding. In all thy ways acknowledge him, and he shall direct thy paths.
                                        Proverbs 3:5-6

He that handleth a matter wisely shall find good: and whoso trusteth in the LORD, happy is he.
                                        Proverbs 16:20

But Daniel purposed in his heart that he would not defile himself with the portion of the king's meat, nor with the wine which he drank: therefore he requested of the prince of the eunuchs that he might not defile himself.   *Daniel 1:8*

Every man according as he purposeth in his heart, so let him give; not grudgingly, or of necessity: for God loveth a cheerful giver.
                                        II Corinthians 9:7

CHAMPIONS MAKE DECISIONS THAT CREATE THE FUTURE THEY DESIRE WHILE LOSERS MAKE DECISIONS THAT CREATE THE PRESENT THEY DESIRE.

DEPRESSION

But thou, O LORD, art a shield for me; my glory, and the lifter up of mine head. I cried unto the LORD with my voice, and he heard me out of his holy hill. I laid me down and slept; I awaked; for the LORD sustained me.   *Psalms 3:3-5*

Weeping may endure for a night, but joy cometh in the morning.   *Psalms 30:5b*

Our soul waiteth for the LORD: he is our help and our shield.   *Psalms 33:20*

Why art thou cast down, O my soul? and why art thou disquieted within me? hope thou in God: for I shall yet praise him, who is the health of my countenance, and my God.   *Psalms 42:11*

The LORD shall preserve thy going out and thy coming in from this time forth, and even for evermore.   *Psalms 121:8*

He healeth the broken in heart, and bindeth up their wounds.   *Psalms 147:3*

STRUGGLE IS THE PROOF YOU HAVE NOT YET BEEN CONQUERED. WARFARE ALWAYS SURROUNDS THE BIRTH OF A MIRACLE.

DESIRE

Delight thyself also in the LORD; and he shall give thee the desires of thine heart.

Psalms 37:4

Lord, all my desire is before thee; and my groaning is not hid from thee. *Psalms 38:9*

There is none upon earth that I desire beside thee.
Psalms 73:25b

The desire accomplished is sweet to the soul:
Proverbs 13:19a

And all things, whatsoever ye shall ask in prayer, believing, ye shall receive. *Matthew 21:22*

Therefore I say unto you, What things soever ye desire, when ye pray, believe that ye receive them, and ye shall have them. *Mark 11:24*

And I say unto you, Ask, and it shall be given you; seek, and ye shall find; knock, and it shall be opened unto you. *Luke 11:9*

THE PROOF OF DESIRE IS PURSUIT. YOU WILL NEVER POSSESS WHAT YOU ARE UNWILLING TO PURSUE. DESIRE IS NOT WHAT YOU WANT IT'S WHAT YOU CANNOT LIVE WITHOUT. WHATEVER YOU ARE SEEKING IS SOMEWHERE SEEKING YOU.

DILIGENCE

He becometh poor that dealeth with a slack hand: but the hand of the diligent maketh rich. He that gathereth in summer is a wise son: but he that sleepeth in harvest is a son that causeth shame.

Proverbs 10:4-5

The hand of the diligent shall bear rule: The substance of a diligent man is precious.

Proverbs 12:24a, 27b

The soul of the sluggard desireth, and hath nothing: but the soul of the diligent shall be made fat.

Proverbs 13:4

Seest thou a man diligent in his business? He shall stand before kings; he shall not stand before mean men. *Proverbs 22:29*

Whatsoever thy hand findeth to do, do it with thy might; for there is no work, nor device, nor knowledge, nor wisdom, in the grave, whither thou goest.

Ecclesiastes 9:10

I can do all things through Christ which strengtheneth me. *Philippians 4:13*

DILIGENCE IS SPEEDY ATTENTION TO AN ASSIGNED TASK. IT IS INSISTENCE UPON COMPLETION.

DISAPPOINTMENT

Have not I commanded thee? Be strong and of a good courage; be not afraid, neither be thou dismayed: for the LORD thy God is with thee whithersoever thou goest.   *Joshua 1:9*

The LORD is my light and my salvation; whom shall I fear? The LORD is the strength of my life; of whom shall I be afraid? When the wicked, even mine enemies and my foes, came upon me to eat up my flesh, they stumbled and fell. Though an host should encamp against me, my heart shall not fear: though war should rise against me, in this will I be confident.   *Psalms 27:1-3*

I will lift up mine eyes unto the hills, from whence cometh my help. My help cometh from the LORD, which made heaven and earth.
              Psalms 121:1-2

And we know that all things work together for good to them that love God, to them who are the called according to his purpose. What shall we then say to these things? If God be for us, who can be against us?   *Romans 8:28, 31*

DISAPPOINTMENT IS MERELY THE SCHOOL OF DISCOVERY.

DISCIPLINE

Teach me to do thy will; for thou art my God: thy spirit is good; lead me into the land of uprightness.
Psalms 143:10

He that spareth his rod hateth his son: but he that loveth him chasteneth him betimes.
Proverbs 13:24

Chasten thy son while there is hope, and let not thy soul spare for his crying.   *Proverbs 19:18*

Train up a child in the way he should go:
and when he is old, he will not depart from it.
Foolishness is bound in the heart of a child; but the rod of correction shall drive it far from him.
Proverbs 22:6, 15

O LORD, correct me, but with judgment; not in thine anger, lest thou bring me to nothing.
Jeremiah 10:24

For whom the Lord loveth he chasteneth, and scourgeth every son whom he receiveth. If ye endure chastening, God dealeth with you as with sons; for what son is he whom the father chasteneth not? But if ye be without chastisement, whereof all are partakers, then are ye bastards, and not sons.
Hebrews 12:6-8

CHAMPIONS ARE WILLING TO DO THINGS THEY HATE TO CREATE SOMETHING THEY LOVE.

DISCRETION

Give therefore thy servant an understanding heart to judge thy people, that I may discern between good and bad: for who is able to judge this thy so great a people?   *I Kings 3:9*

Blessed is the man that walketh not in the counsel of the ungodly, nor standeth in the way of sinners, nor sitteth in the seat of the scornful. But his delight is in the law of the LORD; and in his law doth he meditate day and night. And he shall be like a tree planted by the rivers of water, that bringeth forth his fruit in his season; his leaf also shall not wither; and whatsoever he doeth shall prosper.
Psalms 1:1-3

A good man showeth favour, and lendeth: he will guide his affairs with discretion.   *Psalms 112:5*

I am thy servant; give me understanding, that I may know thy testimonies. The entrance of thy words giveth light; it giveth understanding unto the simple.   *Psalms 119:125, 130*

Trust in the LORD with all thine heart; and lean not unto thine own understanding. In all thy ways acknowledge him, and he shall direct thy paths.
Proverbs 3:5-6

NEVER DISCUSS YOUR PROBLEM WITH SOMEONE WHO CANNOT SOLVE IT. SILENCE CANNOT BE MISQUOTED.

ENTHUSIASM

Let the heavens be glad, and let the earth rejoice: and let men say among the nations, The LORD reigneth.   I Chronicles 16:31

Thou hast turned for me my mourning into dancing: *Psalms 30:11a*

O clap your hands, all ye people; shout unto God with the voice of triumph.   *Psalms 47:1*

Blessed is the people that know the joyful sound: they shall walk, O LORD, in the light of thy countenance.   *Psalms 89:15*

A merry heart maketh a cheerful countenance:.   *Proverbs 15:13a*

For ye shall go out with joy, and be led forth with peace: *Isaiah 55:12a*

Speaking to yourselves in psalms and hymns and spiritual songs, singing and making melody in your heart to the Lord;   *Ephesians 5:19*

ENTHUSIASM IS THE AWARENESS THAT EVERY NEW BEGINNING BEGINS IN DARKNESS.

ETHICS

Thou shalt not bear false witness against
thy neighbour.   *Exodus 20:16*

Blessed is the man that walketh not in the counsel
of the ungodly, nor standeth in the way of sinners,
nor sitteth in the seat of the scornful. But his delight
is in the law of the LORD; and in his law doth he
meditate day and night.   *Psalms 1:1-2*

Let integrity and uprightness preserve me; for I
wait on thee.   *Psalms 25:21*

Judge me, O LORD; for I have walked in mine
integrity: I have trusted also in the LORD; therefore
I shall not slide.

Psalms 26:1

The just man walketh in his integrity: his children
are blessed after him.   *Proverbs 20:7*

Recompense to no man evil for evil. Provide
things honest in the sight of all men.

Romans 12:17

**WHAT YOU ARE IS REVEALED BY WHAT YOU
DO. WHAT YOU DO REVEALS WHAT YOU
REALLY BELIEVE.**

EXCELLENCE

The righteous also shall hold on his way, and he that hath clean hands shall be stronger and stronger.
Job 17:9

The righteous shall flourish like the palm tree: he shall grow like a cedar in Lebanon.
Psalms 92:12

A good name is rather to be chosen than great riches, and loving favour rather than silver and gold.
Proverbs 22:1

Then the presidents and princes sought to find occasion against Daniel concerning the kingdom; but they could find none occasion nor fault; forasmuch as he was faithful, neither was there any error or fault found in him.
Daniel 6:4

Therefore, as ye abound in every thing, in faith, and utterance, and knowledge, and in all diligence, and in your love to us, see that ye abound in this grace also.
II Corinthians 8:7

THE GREATEST QUALITY OF SUCCESS IS THE WILLINGNESS TO BECOME.

EXPECTATION

Why art thou cast down, O my soul? and why art thou disquieted within me? hope thou in God: for I shall yet praise him, who is the health of my countenance, and my God.   *Psalms 42:11*

My soul, wait thou only upon God; for my expectation is from him.   *Psalms 62:5*

For surely there is an end; and thine expectation shall not be cut off.   *Proverbs 23:18*

Jesus said unto him, If thou canst believe, all things are possible to him that believeth.
                                                                         Mark 9:23

For verily I say unto you, That whosoever shall say unto this mountain, Be thou removed, and be thou cast into the sea; and shall not doubt in his heart, but shall believe that those things which he saith shall come to pass; he shall have whatsoever he saith. Therefore I say unto you, What things soever ye desire, when ye pray, believe that ye receive them, and ye shall have them.
                                                                         Mark 11:23-24

But without faith it is impossible to please him: for he that cometh to God must believe that he is, and that he is a rewarder of them that diligently seek him.   *Hebrews 11:6*

THE SEASONS OF YOUR LIFE WILL CHANGE EVERY TIME YOU DECIDE TO USE YOUR FAITH.

FAITH

And all things, whatsoever ye shall ask in prayer, believing, ye shall receive.   *Matthew 21:22*

Jesus said unto him, If thou canst believe, all things are possible to him that believeth.
Mark 9:23

And the Lord said, If ye had faith as a grain of mustard seed, ye might say unto this sycamine tree, Be thou plucked up by the root, and be thou planted in the sea; and it should obey you.
Luke 17:6

Therefore I say unto you, What things soever ye desire, when ye pray, believe that ye receive them, and ye shall have them.   *Mark 11:24*

He staggered not at the promise of God through unbelief; but was strong in faith, giving glory to God; And being fully persuaded that, what he had promised, he was able also to perform.
Romans 4:20-21

Above all, taking the shield of faith, wherewith ye shall be able to quench all the fiery darts of the wicked.   *Ephesians 6:16*

WHEN YOU WANT SOMETHING YOU'VE NEVER HAD YOU'VE GOT TO DO SOMETHING YOU'VE NEVER DONE.

FAMILY

Train up a child in the way he should go: and when he is old, he will not depart from it.

Proverbs 22:6

The father of the righteous shall greatly rejoice: and he that begetteth a wise child shall have joy of him. *Proverbs 23:24*

Through wisdom is an house builded; and by understanding it is established:

Proverbs 24:3

And all thy children shall be taught of the LORD; and great shall be the peace of thy children.

Isaiah 54:13

And they said, Believe on the Lord Jesus Christ, and thou shalt be saved, and thy house.

Acts 16:31

And, ye fathers, provoke not your children to wrath: but bring them up in the nurture and admonition of the Lord. *Ephesians 6:4*

But if any provide not for his own, and specially for those of his own house, he hath denied the faith, and is worse than an infidel. *I Timothy 5:8*

YOU ARE THE SEED THAT DECIDES THE HARVEST AROUND YOU.

FAVOR

A good man showeth favour, and lendeth: he will guide his affairs with discretion.

Psalms 112:5

He that diligently seeketh good procureth favour: but he that seeketh mischief, it shall come unto him.

Proverbs 11:27

A good man obtaineth favour of the LORD: but a man of wicked devices will he condemn.

Proverbs 12:2

Good understanding giveth favour: but the way of transgressors is hard. Every prudent man dealeth with knowledge: but a fool layeth open his folly

Proverbs 13:15-16

Favour is deceitful, and beauty is vain: but a woman that feareth the LORD, she shall be praised.

Proverbs 31:30

And Jesus increased in wisdom and stature, and in favour with God and man.   *Luke 2:52*

CURRENTS OF FAVOR BEGIN TO FLOW THE MOMENT YOU SOLVE A PROBLEM FOR SOMEONE.

FEAR

Be strong and of a good courage, fear not, nor be afraid of them: for the LORD thy God, he it is that doth go with thee; he will not fail thee, nor forsake thee. *Deuteronomy 31:6*

Behold, God is my salvation; I will trust, and not be afraid: for the LORD JEHOVAH is my strength and my song; he also is become my salvation.
Isaiah 12:2

Fear thou not; for I am with thee: be not dismayed; for I am thy God: I will strengthen thee; yea, I will help thee; yea, I will uphold thee with the right hand of my righteousness. *Isaiah 41:10*

For ye have not received the spirit of bondage again to fear; but ye have received the Spirit of adoption, whereby we cry, Abba, Father.
Romans 8:15

For God hath not given us the spirit of fear; but of power, and of love, and of a sound mind.
II Timothy 1:7

EXAMINE WELL WHAT YOU'RE RUNNING FROM. YOU ARE NOT PREY. YOUR FUTURE IS WHIMPERING AT YOUR FEET BEGGING FOR INSTRUCTIONS.

FOCUS

My heart is fixed, O God, my heart is fixed: I will sing and give praise.
Psalms 57:7

I press toward the mark for the prize of the high calling of God in Christ Jesus.
Philippians 3:14

Only be thou strong and very courageous, that thou mayest observe to do according to all the law, which Moses my servant commanded thee: turn not from it to the right hand or to the left, that thou mayest prosper whithersoever thou goest.
Joshua 1:7

And Jesus said unto him, No man, having put his hand to the plow, and looking back, is fit for the kingdom of God.
Luke 9:62

But if from thence thou shalt seek the LORD thy God, thou shalt find him, if thou seek him with all thy heart and with all thy soul.
Deuteronomy 4:29

Ye shall observe to do therefore as the LORD your God hath commanded you: ye shall not turn aside to the right hand or to the left.
Deuteronomy 5:32

THE ONLY REASON MEN FAIL IS BROKEN FOCUS. YOU WILL ONLY HAVE SIGNIFICANT SUCCESS WITH SOMETHING THAT IS OBSESSION.

FORGIVENESS

The discretion of a man deferreth his anger; and it is his glory to pass over a transgression.

Proverbs 19:11

If thine enemy be hungry, give him bread to eat: and if he be thirsty, give him water to drink:

Proverbs 25:21

Blessed are the merciful: for they shall obtain mercy.   Matthew 5:7

But I say unto you, That ye resist not evil: but whosoever shall smite thee on thy right cheek, turn to him the other also.   *Matthew 5:39*

But if ye forgive not men their trespasses, neither will your Father forgive your trespasses.

Matthew 6:15

And be ye kind one to another, tenderhearted, forgiving one another, even as God for Christ's sake hath forgiven you.   *Ephesians 4:32*

Forbearing one another, and forgiving one another,

Colossians 3:13a

MERCY IS LIKE MONEY. YOUR DEPOSITS DETERMINE YOUR WITHDRAWALS.

FRIENDSHIP

Behold, how good and how pleasant it is for brethren to dwell together in unity!

Psalms 133:1

A friend loveth at all times, and a brother is born for adversity

Proverbs 17:17

A man that hath friends must show himself friendly: and there is a friend that sticketh closer than a brother.

Proverbs 18:24

Make no friendship with an angry man;

Proverbs 22:24a

Faithful are the wounds of a friend; but the kisses of an enemy are deceitful. Ointment and perfume rejoice the heart: so doth the sweetness of a man's friend by hearty counsel. Thine own friend, and thy father's friend, forsake not; neither go into thy brother's house in the day of thy calamity: for better is a neighbour that is near than a brother far off.

Proverbs 27:6, 9-10

Greater love hath no man than this, that a man lay down his life for his friends. Ye are my friends, if ye do whatsoever I command you.

John 15:13-14

WHEN GOD WANTS TO BLESS YOU, HE PUTS A PERSON IN YOUR LIFE.

GOAL SETTING

In all thy ways acknowledge him, and he shall direct thy paths.   *Proverbs 3:6*

The preparations of the heart in man, and the answer of the tongue, is from the LORD. A man's heart deviseth his way: but the LORD directeth his steps.   *Proverbs 16:1, 9*

For which of you, intending to build a tower, sitteth not down first, and counteth the cost, whether he have sufficient to finish it? Lest haply, after he hath laid the foundation, and is not able to finish it, all that behold it begin to mock him, Saying, This man began to build, and was not able to finish. Or what king, going to make war against another king, sitteth not down first, and consulteth whether he be able with ten thousand to meet him that cometh against him with twenty thousand Or else, while the other is yet a great way off, he sendeth an ambassage, and desireth conditions of peace.

Luke 14:28-32

Go to the ant, thou sluggard; consider her ways, and be wise: Which having no guide, overseer, or ruler, Provideth her meat in the summer, and gathereth her food in the harvest.   Proverbs 6:6-8

YOU WILL NEVER LEAVE WHERE YOU ARE UNTIL YOU DECIDE WHERE YOU WOULD RATHER BE.

GOD

In the beginning God created the heaven and the earth.
Genesis 1:1

In the beginning was the Word, and the Word was with God, and the Word was God. The same was in the beginning with God.
John 1:1-2

For it is written, As I live, saith the Lord, every knee shall bow to me, and every tongue shall confess to God. So then every one of us shall give account of himself to God.
Romans 14:11-12

For by him were all things created, that are in heaven, and that are in earth, visible and invisible, whether they be thrones, or dominions, or principalities, or powers: all things were created by him, and for him: And he is before all things, and by him all things consist.
Colossians 1:16-17

And a voice came out of the throne, saying, Praise our God, all ye his servants, and ye that fear him, both small and great.
Revelation 19:5

The fool hath said in his heart, There is no God. Corrupt are they, and have done abominable iniquity: there is none that doeth good.
Psalms 53:1

THE EVIDENCE OF GOD'S PRESENCE FAR OUTWEIGHS THE PROOF OF HIS ABSENCE.

GOSSIP

Whoso privily slandereth his neighbour, him will
I cut off: him that hath an high look and a proud
heart will not I suffer.   *Psalms 101:5*

Set a watch, O LORD, before my mouth; keep the
door of my lips.   *Psalms 141:3*

For by thy words thou shalt be justified, and by
thy words thou shalt be condemned.
                                            Matthew 12:37

Let no corrupt communication proceed out of
your mouth, but that which is good to the use of edifying, that it may minister grace unto the hearers.
                                            Ephesians 4:29

And withal they learn to be idle, wandering about
from house to house; and not only idle, but tattlers
also and busybodies, speaking things which they
ought not.   *I Timothy 5:13*

But let none of you suffer as a murderer, or as a
thief, or as an evildoer, or as a busybody in other
men's matters.   *I Peter 4:15*

Wherefore, my beloved brethren, let every man be
swift to hear, slow to speak, slow to wrath:
                                            James 1:19

**FALSE ACCUSATION IS THE LAST STAGE BEFORE
SUPERNATURAL PROMOTION.**

GRATITUDE

Enter into his gates with thanksgiving, and into his courts with praise: be thankful unto him, and bless his name.   *Psalms 100:4*

And he took the cup, and gave thanks, and said, Take this, and divide it among yourselves: And he took bread, and gave thanks, and brake it, and gave unto them, saying, This is my body which is given for you: this do in remembrance of me.
                                   Luke 22:17, 19

Blessed be the God and Father of our Lord Jesus Christ, who hath blessed us with all spiritual blessings in heavenly places in Christ: *Ephesians 1:3*

Giving thanks always for all things unto God and the Father in the name of our Lord Jesus Christ;
                                   Ephesians 5:20

Be careful for nothing; but in every thing by prayer and supplication with thanksgiving let your requests be made known unto God.
                                   Philippians 4:6

Blessing, and glory, and wisdom, and thanksgiving, and honour, and power, and might, be unto our God for ever and ever. Amen.   *Revelation 7:12b*

GRATITUDE IS SIMPLY AWARENESS OF THE GIVERS IN YOUR LIFE. YOU CAN NOT NAME ONE THING THAT WAS NOT GIVEN TO YOU.

GREED

There is that scattereth, and yet increaseth; and there is that withholdeth more than is meet, but it tendeth to poverty. The liberal soul shall be made fat: and he that watereth shall be watered also himself.

Proverbs 11:24-25

He that despiseth his neighbour sinneth: but he that hath mercy on the poor, happy is he.

Proverbs 14:21

He that is greedy of gain troubleth his own house;

Proverbs 15:27a

And he said unto them, Take heed, and beware of covetousness: for a man's life consisteth not in the abundance of the things which he possesseth. For where your treasure is, there will your heart be also.

Luke 12:15, 34

Be content with such things as ye have: for he hath said, I will never leave thee, nor forsake thee.

Hebrews 13:5b

Labour not to be rich: cease from thine own wisdom. Wilt thou set thine eyes upon that which is not? for riches certainly make themselves wings; they fly away as an eagle toward heaven.

Proverbs 23:4-5

GIVING IS THE ONLY PROOF THAT YOU HAVE OVERCOME GREED.

HABITS

So will I sing praise unto thy name for ever, that I may daily perform my vows.   *Psalms 61:8*

My son, keep my words, and lay up my commandments with thee.   *Proverbs 7:1*

Know ye not, that to whom ye yield yourselves servants to obey, his servants ye are to whom ye obey; whether of sin unto death, or of obedience unto righteousness?   *Romans 6:16*

This I say then, Walk in the Spirit, and ye shall not fulfil the lust of the flesh.   *Galatians 5:16*

I can do all things through Christ which strengtheneth me.   *Philippians 4:13*

Howbeit for this cause I obtained mercy, that in me first Jesus Christ might show forth all longsuffering, for a pattern to them which should hereafter believe on him to life everlasting.
          I Timothy 1:16

In all things showing thyself a pattern of good works: in doctrine showing uncorruptness, gravity, sincerity,   *Titus 2:7*

MEN DO NOT DECIDE THEIR FUTURE. THEY DECIDE THEIR HABITS AND THEIR HABITS DECIDE THEIR FUTURE. THE SECRET OF YOUR FUTURE IS HIDDEN IN YOUR DAILY ROUTINE.

HAPPINESS

Behold, happy is the man whom God correcteth: therefore despise not thou the chastening of the Almighty: *Job 5:17*

Thou hast put gladness in my heart, more than in the time that their corn and their wine increased.
Psalms 4:7

Happy is that people, that is in such a case: yea, happy is that people, whose God is the LORD.
Psalms 144:15

He that despiseth his neighbour sinneth: but he that hath mercy on the poor, happy is he.
Proverbs 14:21

He that handleth a matter wisely shall find good: and whoso trusteth in the LORD, happy is he.
Proverbs 16:20

He that keepeth the law, happy is he.
Proverbs 29:18

Happy is the man that findeth wisdom, and the man that getteth understanding.
Proverbs 3:13

HAPPY IS THE MAN THAT FINDETH WISDOM. THAT IS HOW YOU KNOW WHO HAS IT.

HEALTH

He healeth the broken in heart, and bindeth up
their wounds.   *Psalms 147:3*

Be not wise in thine own eyes: fear the LORD,
and depart from evil. It shall be health to thy navel,
and marrow to thy bones.   *Proverbs 3:7-8*

My son, attend to my words; incline thine ear
unto my sayings. Let them not depart from thine
eyes; keep them in the midst of thine heart. For
they are life unto those that find them, and health to
all their flesh.   *Proverbs 4:20-22*

Pleasant words are as an honeycomb, sweet to the
soul, and health to the bones.   *Proverbs 16:24*

A merry heart doeth good like a medicine: but a
broken spirit drieth the bones.   *Proverbs 17:22*

Beloved, I wish above all things that thou mayest
prosper and be in health, even as thy soul prospereth.
                                       III John 1:2

I will put none of these diseases upon thee, which
I have brought upon the Egyptians: for I am the
LORD that healeth thee.   *Exodus 15:26b*

For I will restore health unto thee, and I will heal
thee of thy wounds, saith the LORD;
                                       Jeremiah 30:17a

LONGEVITY IS THE PRODUCT OF WISDOM.

42

HUMILITY

By humility and the fear of the LORD are riches, and honour, and life. *Proverbs 22:4*

Whosoever therefore shall humble himself as this little child, the same is greatest in the kingdom of heaven. *Matthew 18:4*

Put on therefore, as the elect of God, holy and beloved, bowels of mercies, kindness, humbleness of mind, meekness, longsuffering;

Colossians 3:12

And being found in fashion as a man, he humbled himself, and became obedient unto death, even the death of the cross. *Philippians 2:8*

Humble yourselves therefore under the mighty hand of God, that he may exalt you in due time:

I Peter 5:6

But he giveth more grace. Wherefore he saith, God resisteth the proud, but giveth grace unto the humble. Humble yourselves in the sight of the Lord, and he shall lift you up. *James 4:6, 10*

THOSE IN HIGH PLACES CAN BE BROUGHT DOWN. THOSE IN LOW PLACES CAN BE CALLED UP. HUMILITY IS THE AWARENESS OF IT.

43

IGNORANCE

Give therefore thy servant an understanding heart to judge thy people, that I may discern between good and bad: for who is able to judge this thy so great a people?   *I Kings 3:9*

The fear of the LORD is the beginning of wisdom: a good understanding have all they that do his commandments: his praise endureth for ever.
Psalms 111:10

For the LORD giveth wisdom: out of his mouth cometh knowledge and understanding. He layeth up sound wisdom for the righteous: he is a buckler to them that walk uprightly.   *Proverbs 2:6-7*

For this cause we also, since the day we heard it, do not cease to pray for you, and to desire that ye might be filled with the knowledge of his will in all wisdom and spiritual understanding; That ye might walk worthy of the Lord unto all pleasing, being fruitful in every good work, and increasing in the knowledge of God;   *Colossians 1:9-10*

My people are destroyed for lack of knowledge: because thou hast rejected knowledge, I will also reject thee, that thou shalt be no priest to me: seeing thou hast forgotten the law of thy God, I will also forget thy children.   *Hosea 4:6*

YOU WILL NEVER CHANGE WHAT YOU BELIEVE UNTIL YOUR BELIEF SYSTEM CANNOT PRODUCE SOMETHING YOU WANT.

INFORMATION

The entrance of thy words giveth light; it giveth understanding unto the simple.

Psalms 119:130

Whoso loveth instruction loveth knowledge: but he that hateth reproof is brutish.

Proverbs 12:1

For God giveth to a man that is good in his sight wisdom, and knowledge, and joy:

Ecclesiastes 2:26a

My people are destroyed for lack of knowledge: because thou hast rejected knowledge, I will also reject thee, that thou shalt be no priest to me: seeing thou hast forgotten the law of thy God, I will also forget thy children.   *Hosea 4:6*

For this cause we also, since the day we heard it, do not cease to pray for you, and to desire that ye might be filled with the knowledge of his will in all wisdom and spiritual understanding; That ye might walk worthy of the Lord unto all pleasing, being fruitful in every good work, and increasing in the knowledge of God;   *Colossians 1:9-10*

THE DIFFERENCE IN PEOPLE IS BETWEEN THEIR EARS. THE DIFFERENCE BETWEEN YOUR PRESENT AND YOUR FUTURE IS INFORMATION.

INTEGRITY

Let me be weighed in an even balance that God may know mine integrity.   *Job 31:6*

Blessed is the man that walketh not in the counsel of the ungodly, nor standeth in the way of sinners, nor sitteth in the seat of the scornful.

Psalms 1:1

The fear of the LORD is the beginning of wisdom: a good understanding have all they that do his commandments: his praise endureth for ever.

Psalms 111:10

A good man showeth favour, and lendeth: he will guide his affairs with discretion.

Psalms 112:5

The just man walketh in his integrity: his children are blessed after him.   *Proverbs 20:7*

But if ye have bitter envying and strife in your hearts, glory not, and lie not against the truth.

James 3:14

NEVER REWRITE YOUR THEOLOGY TO ACCOMMODATE A DESIRE.

JESUS

And she shall bring forth a son, and thou shalt call his name JESUS: for he shall save his people from their sins.   *Matthew 1:21*

For unto you is born this day in the city of David a Saviour, which is Christ the Lord.   *Luke 2:11*

Then spake Jesus again unto them, saying, I am the light of the world: he that followeth me shall not walk in darkness, but shall have the light of life.
John 8:12

I am the good shepherd: the good shepherd giveth his life for the sheep.   *John 10:11*

Jesus said unto her, I am the resurrection, and the life: he that believeth in me, though he were dead, yet shall he live: *John 11:25*

Jesus saith unto him, I am the way, the truth, and the life: no man cometh unto the Father, but by me.
John 14:6

For there is one God, and one mediator between God and men, the man Christ Jesus;
I Timothy 2:5

HIS MIND IS KEENER THAN YOURS; HIS MEMORY IS LONGER THAN YOURS; HIS SHOULDERS ARE BIGGER THAN YOURS.

LEADERSHIP

The steps of a good man are ordered by the LORD: and he delighteth in his way.
Psalms 37:23

For the LORD God is a sun and shield: the LORD will give grace and glory: no good thing will he withhold from them that walk uprightly.
Psalms 84:11

For with what judgment ye judge, ye shall be judged: and with what measure ye mete, it shall be measured to you again. *Matthew 7:2*

For as many as are led by the Spirit of God, they are the sons of God. *Romans 8:14*

And the things that thou hast heard of me among many witnesses, the same commit thou to faithful men, who shall be able to teach others also.
II Timothy 2:2

Let the elders that rule well be counted worthy of double honour, especially they who labour in the word and doctrine. For the scripture saith, Thou shalt not muzzle the ox that treadeth out the corn. And, The labourer is worthy of his reward. Against an elder receive not an accusation, but before two or three witnesses. Them that sin rebuke before all, that others also may fear. *I Timothy 5:17-20*

THE ABILITY TO FOLLOW IS THE FIRST QUALIFICATION FOR LEADERSHIP.

LONELINESS

And, behold, I am with thee, and will keep thee in all places whither thou goest, and will bring thee again into this land; for I will not leave thee, until I have done that which I have spoken to thee of.

Genesis 28:15

And the LORD, he it is that doth go before thee; he will be with thee, he will not fail thee, neither forsake thee: fear not, neither be dismayed.

Deuteronomy 31:8

Yea, though I walk through the valley of the shadow of death, I will fear no evil: for thou art with me; thy rod and thy staff they comfort me.

Psalms 23:4

When my father and my mother forsake me, then the LORD will take me up.   Psalms 27:10

I will not leave you comfortless: I will come to you.   John 14:18

I will never leave thee, nor forsake thee.

Hebrews 13:5b

Casting all your care upon him; for he careth for you.   I Peter 5:7

LONELINESS IS NOT THE ABSENCE OF AFFECTION, BUT THE ABSENCE OF DIRECTION.

LOVE

Many waters cannot quench love, neither can the floods drown it: if a man would give all the substance of his house for love, it would utterly be contemned.   *Song of Solomon 8:7*

A new commandment I give unto you, That ye love one another; as I have loved you, that ye also love one another. By this shall all men know that ye are my disciples, if ye have love one to another.
John 13:34-35

For the Father himself loveth you, because ye have loved me, and have believed that I came out from God.   *John 16:27*

For this is the message that ye heard from the beginning, that we should love one another.
I John 3:11

Beloved, let us love one another: for love is of God; and every one that loveth is born of God, and knoweth God. Herein is love, not that we loved God, but that he loved us, and sent his Son to be the propitiation for our sins.   *I John 4:7, 10*

WHAT YOU RESPECT YOU WILL ATTRACT, WHAT YOU DON'T RESPECT WILL MOVE AWAY FROM YOU.

LOYALTY

Be strong and of a good courage, fear not, nor be afraid of them: for the LORD thy God, he it is that doth go with thee; he will not fail thee, nor forsake thee.   *Deuteronomy 31:6*

A good man showeth favour, and lendeth: he will guide his affairs with discretion.
Psalms 112:5

Blessed are they that keep his testimonies, and that seek him with the whole heart. Thou hast commanded us to keep thy precepts diligently.
Psalms 119:2, 4

Discretion shall preserve thee, understanding shall keep thee: *Proverbs 2:11*

A man that hath friends must show himself friendly: and there is a friend that sticketh closer than a brother.   *Proverbs 18:24*

Faithful are the wounds of a friend; but the kisses of an enemy are deceitful.   *Proverbs 27:6*

Recompense to no man evil for evil. Provide things honest in the sight of all men.
Romans 12:17

GIVE ANOTHER WHAT HE CANNOT FIND ANYWHERE ELSE AND HE WILL KEEP RETURNING.

LYING

I have hated them that regard lying vanities: but I trust in the LORD.   *Psalms 31:6*

The lip of truth shall be established for ever: but a lying tongue is but for a moment.
Proverbs 12:19

Blessed are ye, when men shall revile you, and persecute you, and shall say all manner of evil against you falsely, for my sake.
Matthew 5:11

Wherefore putting away lying, speak every man truth with his neighbour: for we are members one of another.   *Ephesians 4:25*

For we know him that hath said, Vengeance belongeth unto me, I will recompense, saith the Lord. And again, The Lord shall judge his people.
Hebrews 10:30

But the fearful, and unbelieving, and the abominable, and murderers, and whoremongers, and sorcerers, and idolaters, and all liars, shall have their part in the lake which burneth with fire and brimstone: which is the second death.
Revelation 21:8

THOSE WHO WILL LIE FOR YOU EVENTUALLY WILL LIE ABOUT YOU. THOSE WHO SIN WITH YOU WILL EVENTUALLY SIN AGAINST YOU.

MENTORSHIP

And he gave some, apostles; and some, prophets; and some, evangelists; and some, pastors and teachers; For the perfecting of the saints, for the work of the ministry, for the edifying of the body of Christ:

Ephesians 4:11-12

Study to show thyself approved unto God, a workman that needeth not to be ashamed, rightly dividing the word of truth.   *II Timothy 2:15*

When I call to remembrance the unfeigned faith that is in thee, which dwelt first in thy grandmother Lois, and thy mother Eunice; and I am persuaded that in thee also. Wherefore I put thee in remembrance that thou stir up the gift of God, which is in thee by the putting on of my hands.

II Timothy 1:5-6

And Joshua the son of Nun was full of the spirit of wisdom; for Moses had laid his hands upon him: and the children of Israel hearkened unto him, and did as the LORD commanded Moses.

Deuteronomy 34:9

SOMEONE HAS HEARD WHAT YOU HAVE NOT; SOMEONE HAS SEEN WHAT YOU HAVE NOT; SOMEONE KNOWS WHAT YOU DO NOT. YOUR SUCCESS DEPENDS ON YOUR WILLINGNESS TO BE MENTORED BY THEM.

MIRACLES

Ask, and it shall be given you; seek, and ye shall find; knock, and it shall be opened unto you:

Matthew 7:7

How God anointed Jesus of Nazareth with the Holy Ghost and with power: who went about doing good, and healing all that were oppressed of the devil; for God was with him. *Acts 10:38*

And these signs shall follow them that believe; In my name shall they cast out devils; they shall speak with new tongues; They shall take up serpents; and if they drink any deadly thing, it shall not hurt them; they shall lay hands on the sick, and they shall recover. *Mark 16:17-18*

For verily I say unto you, That whosoever shall say unto this mountain, Be thou removed, and be thou cast into the sea; and shall not doubt in his heart, but shall believe that those things which he saith shall come to pass; he shall have whatsoever he saith. Therefore I say unto you, What things soever ye desire, when ye pray, believe that ye receive them, and ye shall have them. *Mark 11:23-24*

Ah Lord GOD! behold, thou hast made the heaven and the earth by thy great power and stretched out arm, and there is nothing too hard for thee:

Jeremiah 32:17

YOU'RE NEVER AS FAR FROM A MIRACLE AS IT FIRST APPEARS.

MOTIVATION

Be strong and of a good courage, fear not, nor be afraid of them: for the LORD thy God, he it is that doth go with thee; he will not fail thee, nor forsake thee.   *Deuteronomy 31:6*

Have not I commanded thee? Be strong and of a good courage; be not afraid, neither be thou dismayed: for the LORD thy God is with thee whithersoever thou goest.   *Joshua 1:9*

And he answered, Fear not: for they that be with us are more than they that be with them.
                                             II Kings 6:16

Through thee will we push down our enemies: through thy name will we tread them under that rise up against us.   *Psalms 44:5*

Therefore I will look unto the LORD; I will wait for the God of my salvation: my God will hear me. When I sit in darkness, the LORD shall be a light unto me.   *Micah 7:7, 8b*

I can do all things through Christ which strengtheneth me.   *Philippians 4:13*

DISCONTENTMENT IS THE CATALYST FOR CHANGE. INTOLERANCE OF THE PRESENT CREATES A FUTURE.

OBEDIENCE

Now therefore, if ye will obey my voice indeed, and keep my covenant, then ye shall be a peculiar treasure unto me above all people: for all the earth is mine: *Exodus 19:5*

But if thou shalt indeed obey his voice, and do all that I speak; then I will be an enemy unto thine enemies, and an adversary unto thine adversaries. For mine Angel shall go before thee,
                              Exodus 23:22-23a

If ye be willing and obedient, ye shall eat the good of the land: *Isaiah 1:19*

Whether it be good, or whether it be evil, we will obey the voice of the LORD our God,
                              Jeremiah 42:6a

Children, obey your parents in the Lord: for this is right.   *Ephesians 6:1*

For as by one man's disobedience many were made sinners, so by the obedience of one shall many be made righteous.   *Romans 5:19*

Casting down imaginations, and every high thing that exalteth itself against the knowledge of God, and bringing into captivity every thought to the obedience of Christ;   *II Corinthians 10:5*

GOD WILL NEVER ADVANCE YOU BEYOND YOUR LAST ACT OF DISOBEDIENCE.

OPPOSITION

Rest in the LORD, and wait patiently for him: fret not thyself because of him who prospereth in his way, because of the man who bringeth wicked devices to pass.   Psalms 37:7

In my distress I cried unto the LORD, and he heard me. Deliver my soul, O LORD, from lying lips, and from a deceitful tongue.
                                            Psalms 120:1-2

No weapon that is formed against thee shall prosper; and every tongue that shall rise against thee in judgment thou shalt condemn. This is the heritage of the servants of the LORD, and their righteousness is of me, saith the LORD.   Isaiah 54:17

When the enemy shall come in like a flood, the Spirit of the LORD shall lift up a standard against him.   Isaiah 59:19b

And who is he that will harm you, if ye be followers of that which is good?   I Peter 3:13

Casting all your care upon him; for he careth for you.   I Peter 5:7

OPPOSITION IS REALLY THE PROOF OF PROGRESS. SATAN ALWAYS ATTACKS THOSE NEXT IN LINE FOR A PROMOTION.

OVERCOMING

Be not overcome of evil, but overcome evil with good.   *Romans 12:21*

I write unto you, young men, because ye have overcome the wicked one. I write unto you, little children, because ye have known the Father.
                    I John 2:13b

Ye are of God, little children, and have overcome them: because greater is he that is in you, than he that is in the world.   *I John 4:4*

To him that overcometh will I give to eat of the tree of life, which is in the midst of the paradise of God.   *Revelation 2:7b*

To him that overcometh will I grant to sit with me in my throne, even as I also overcame, and am set down with my Father in his throne.
                    Revelation 3:21

He that overcometh shall inherit all things; and I will be his God, and he shall be my son.
                    Revelation 21:7

WHAT YOU FAIL TO MASTER IN YOUR LIFE WILL EVENTUALLY MASTER YOU.

PAIN

Look upon mine affliction and my pain; and forgive all my sins.   *Psalms 25:18*

Many are the afflictions of the righteous: but the LORD delivereth him out of them all.

Psalms 34:19

Deliver me from the oppression of man:
Psalms 119:134a

He healeth the broken in heart, and bindeth up their wounds.   *Psalms 147:3*

And one shall say unto him, What are these wounds in thine hands? Then he shall answer, Those with which I was wounded in the house of my friends.   *Zechariah 13:6*

And God shall wipe away all tears from their eyes; and there shall be no more death, neither sorrow, nor crying, neither shall there be any more pain: for the former things are passed away.

Revelation 21:4

PAIN IS DISCOMFORT CREATED BY DISORDER. IT IS NOT YOUR ENEMY BUT MERELY THE PROOF THAT ONE EXISTS.

PATIENCE

Rest in the LORD, and wait patiently for him: fret not thyself because of him who prospereth in his way, because of the man who bringeth wicked devices to pass. *Psalms 37:7*

I waited patiently for the LORD; and he inclined unto me, and heard my cry. *Psalms 40:1*

And not only so, but we glory in tribulations also: knowing that tribulation worketh patience; And patience, experience; and experience, hope: And hope maketh not ashamed; because the love of God is shed abroad in our hearts by the Holy Ghost which is given unto us. *Romans 5:3-5*

Rejoicing in hope; patient in tribulation; continuing instant in prayer; *Romans 12:12*

And let us not be weary in well doing: for in due season we shall reap, if we faint not.
Galatians 6:9

Knowing this, that the trying of your faith worketh patience. But let patience have her perfect work, that ye may be perfect and entire, wanting nothing.
James 1:3-4

PATIENCE IS THE WEAPON THAT FORCES DECEPTION TO REVEAL ITSELF.

PEACE

I will both lay me down in peace, and sleep: for thou, LORD, only makest me dwell in safety.

Psalms 4:8

Great peace have they which love thy law: and nothing shall offend them. *Psalms 119:165*

Thou wilt keep him in perfect peace, whose mind is stayed on thee: because he trusteth in thee. LORD, thou wilt ordain peace for us: for thou also hast wrought all our works in us.

Isaiah 26:3, 12

Peace I leave with you, my peace I give unto you: not as the world giveth, give I unto you. Let not your heart be troubled, neither let it be afraid.

John 14:27

For to be carnally minded is death; but to be spiritually minded is life and peace. *Romans 8:6*

But the fruit of the Spirit is love, joy, peace, longsuffering, gentleness, goodness, faith,

Galatians 5:22

And the fruit of righteousness is sown in peace of them that make peace. *James 3:18*

PEACE IS NOT THE ABSENCE OF CONFLICT, IT'S THE ABSENCE OF INNER CONFLICT.

PEER PRESSURE

If thy brother, the son of thy mother, or thy son, or thy daughter, or the wife of thy bosom, or thy friend, which is as thine own soul, entice thee secretly, saying, Let us go and serve other gods, which thou hast not known, thou, nor thy fathers; Thou shalt not consent unto him, nor hearken unto him; neither shall thine eye pity him, neither shalt thou spare, neither shalt thou conceal him: *Deuteronomy 13:6, 8*

My son, if sinners entice thee, consent thou not. If they say, Come with us, let us lay wait for blood, let us lurk privily for the innocent without cause: Let us swallow them up alive as the grave; and whole, as those that go down into the pit: We shall find all precious substance, we shall fill our houses with spoil: Cast in thy lot among us; let us all have one purse: My son, walk not thou in the way with them; refrain thy foot from their path:
Proverbs 1:10-15

For we have not an high priest which cannot be touched with the feeling of our infirmities; but was in all points tempted like as we are, yet without sin. Let us therefore come boldly unto the throne of grace, that we may obtain mercy, and find grace to help in time of need. *Hebrews 4:15-16*

SATAN'S FAVORITE ENTRY POINT INTO YOUR LIFE IS ALWAYS THROUGH SOMEONE CLOSE TO YOU.

PERSEVERANCE

But he knoweth the way that I take: when he hath tried me, I shall come forth as gold. My foot hath held his steps, his way have I kept, and not declined.
Job 23:10-11

And ye shall be hated of all men for my name's sake: but he that endureth to the end shall be saved.
Matthew 10:22

Then said Jesus to those Jews which believed on him, If ye continue in my word, then are ye my disciples indeed;
John 8:31

As the Father hath loved me, so have I loved you: continue ye in my love.
John 15:9

Confirming the souls of the disciples, and exhorting them to continue in the faith, and that we must through much tribulation enter into the kingdom of God.
Acts 14:22

And he that overcometh, and keepeth my works unto the end, to him will I give power over the nations:
Revelation 2:26

ALL MEN FAIL BUT THE GREAT ONES GET BACK UP.

PLANNING

In all thy ways acknowledge him, and he shall direct thy paths. *Proverbs 3:6*

Without counsel purposes are disappointed: but in the multitude of counsellors they are established. *Proverbs 15:22*

The preparations of the heart in man, and the answer of the tongue, is from the LORD. A man's heart deviseth his way: but the LORD directeth his steps. *Proverbs 16:1, 9*

There are many devices in a man's heart; nevertheless the counsel of the LORD, that shall stand. *Proverbs 19:21*

The thoughts of the diligent tend only to plenteousness; but of every one that is hasty only to want. *Proverbs 21:5*

But the liberal deviseth liberal things; and by liberal things shall he stand *Isaiah 32:8*

For I know the thoughts that I think toward you, saith the LORD, thoughts of peace, and not of evil, to give you an expected end. *Jeremiah 29:11*

THE SEASON FOR RESEARCH IS NOT THE SEASON FOR MARKETING.

PRAYER

Seek the LORD and his strength, seek his face continually. *I Chronicles 16:11*

If my people, which are called by my name, shall humble themselves, and pray, and seek my face, and turn from their wicked ways; then will I hear from heaven, and will forgive their sin, and will heal their land. *II Chronicles 7:14*

Watch and pray, that ye enter not into temptation: the spirit indeed is willing, but the flesh is weak. *Matthew 26:41*

Continue in prayer, and watch in the same with thanksgiving; *Colossians 4:2*

Pray without ceasing. *I Thessalonians 5:17*

The effectual fervent prayer of a righteous man availeth much. *James 5:16b*

But ye, beloved, building up yourselves on your most holy faith, praying in the Holy Ghost, *Jude 1:20*

ONE HOUR IN THE PRESENCE OF GOD WILL REVEAL ANY FLAW IN YOUR MOST CAREFULLY LAID PLANS.

PROBLEM SOLVING

For we have not an high priest which cannot be touched with the feeling of our infirmities; but was in all points tempted like as we are, yet without sin. Let us therefore come boldly unto the throne of grace, that we may obtain mercy, and find grace to help in time of need.   *Hebrews 4:15-16*

He that handleth a matter wisely shall find good: and whoso trusteth in the LORD, happy is he.
                                        Proverbs 16:20

For which of you, intending to build a tower, sitteth not down first, and counteth the cost, whether he have sufficient to finish it?   *Luke 14:28*

Without counsel purposes are disappointed: but in the multitude of counsellors they are established.
                                        Proverbs 15:22

And if we know that he hear us, whatsoever we ask, we know that we have the petitions that we desired of him.   *I John 5:15*

YOU WILL ONLY BE REMEMBERED IN LIFE BY THE PROBLEMS YOU SOLVE AND THE ONES YOU CREATE. YOU WILL ONLY BE PURSUED FOR THE PROBLEMS YOU SOLVE. THE PROBLEM THAT INFURIATES YOU THE MOST IS THE PROBLEM GOD HAS ASSIGNED YOU TO SOLVE.

PRODUCTIVITY

Except the LORD build the house, they labour in vain that build it: except the LORD keep the city, the watchman waketh but in vain.   *Psalms 127:1*

A wise man will hear, and will increase learning; and a man of understanding shall attain unto wise counsels: *Proverbs 1:5*

And other fell on good ground, and did yield fruit that sprang up and increased; and brought forth, some thirty, and some sixty, and some an hundred.
                                                                                 Mark 4:8

Verily, verily, I say unto you, Except a corn of wheat fall into the ground and die, it abideth alone: but if it die, it bringeth forth much fruit.
                                                                                 John 12:24

I am the vine, ye are the branches: He that abideth in me, and I in him, the same bringeth forth much fruit: for without me ye can do nothing.   Herein is my Father glorified, that ye bear much fruit; so shall ye be my disciples.   *John 15:5,8*

That ye might walk worthy of the Lord unto all pleasing, being fruitful in every good work, and increasing in the knowledge of God;
                                                                          Colossians 1:10

THE QUALITY OF YOUR PREPARATION DETERMINES THE QUALITY OF YOUR PERFORMANCE.

PROMOTION

For I will promote thee unto very great honour, and I will do whatsoever thou sayest unto me: come therefore, I pray thee, curse me this people.
Numbers 22:17

For promotion cometh neither from the east, nor from the west, nor from the south. But God is the judge: he putteth down one, and setteth up another.
Psalms 75:6-7

The wise shall inherit glory: but shame shall be the promotion of fools. *Proverbs 3:35*

Wisdom is the principal thing; therefore get wisdom: and with all thy getting get understanding. Exalt her, and she shall promote thee: she shall bring thee to honour, when thou dost embrace her. She shall give to thine head an ornament of grace: a crown of glory shall she deliver to thee.
Proverbs 4:7-9

O LORD, I know that the way of man is not in himself: it is not in man that walketh to direct his steps. *Jeremiah 10:23*

I press toward the mark for the prize of the high calling of God in Christ Jesus. *Philippians 3:14*

SOMEONE IS ALWAYS OBSERVING YOU WHO IS CAPABLE OF GREATLY BLESSING YOU. YOU WILL NEVER BE PROMOTED UNTIL YOU BECOME OVERQUALIFIED FOR YOUR PRESENT POSITION.

PROSPERITY

If they obey and serve him, they shall spend their days in prosperity, and their years in pleasures.

Job 36:11

Blessed is the man that walketh not in the counsel of the ungodly, nor standeth in the way of sinners, nor sitteth in the seat of the scornful. But his delight is in the law of the LORD; and in his law doth he meditate day and night. And he shall be like a tree planted by the rivers of water, that bringeth forth his fruit in his season; his leaf also shall not wither; and whatsoever he doeth shall prosper.

Psalms 1:1-3

Let the LORD be magnified, which hath pleasure in the prosperity of his servant. *Psalms 35:27b*

Beloved, I wish above all things that thou mayest prosper and be in health, even as thy soul prospereth.

III John 1:2

Ye shall diligently keep the commandments of the LORD your God, and his testimonies, and his statutes, which he hath commanded thee. That thou mayest go in and possess the good land which the LORD sware unto thy fathers,

Deuteronomy 6:17, 18b

PROSPERITY IS HAVING ENOUGH OF GOD'S PROVISION TO COMPLETE HIS INSTRUCTIONS FOR YOUR LIFE.

PROTECTION

Yea, though I walk through the valley of the shadow of death, I will fear no evil: for thou art with me; thy rod and thy staff they comfort me. Thou preparest a table before me in the presence of mine enemies: thou anointest my head with oil; my cup runneth over. *Psalms 23:4-5*

He that dwelleth in the secret place of the most High shall abide under the shadow of the Almighty. He shall cover thee with his feathers, and under his wings shalt thou trust: his truth shall be thy shield and buckler. Thou shalt not be afraid for the terror by night; nor for the arrow that flieth by day; Nor for the pestilence that walketh in darkness; nor for the destruction that wasteth at noonday. A thousand shall fall at thy side, and ten thousand at thy right hand; but it shall not come nigh thee. There shall no evil befall thee, neither shall any plague come nigh thy dwelling. For he shall give his angels charge over thee, to keep thee in all thy ways. *Psalms 91:1, 4-7, 10-11*

And I will rebuke the devourer for your sakes, and he shall not destroy the fruits of your ground; neither shall your vine cast her fruit before the time in the field, saith the LORD of hosts. *Malachi 3:11*

PROTECTION IS PRODUCED THROUGH PARTNERSHIP.

RACISM

A new commandment I give unto you, That ye love one another; as I have loved you, that ye also love one another. John 13:34

There is neither Jew nor Greek, there is neither bond nor free, there is neither male nor female: for ye are all one in Christ Jesus. Galatians 3:28

And walk in love, as Christ also hath loved us, and hath given himself for us an offering and a sacrifice to God for a sweetsmelling savour.

Ephesians 5:2

But he that doeth wrong shall receive for the wrong which he hath done: and there is no respect of persons. Colossians 3:25

If ye fulfil the royal law according to the scripture, Thou shalt love thy neighbour as thyself, ye do well: But if ye have respect to persons, ye commit sin, and are convinced of the law as transgressors.

James 2:8-9

YOUR SIGNIFICANCE IS NOT IN YOUR SIMILARITY TO ANOTHER BUT IN YOUR POINT OF DIFFERENCE FROM ANOTHER.

REPUTATION

Blessed is the man that walketh not in the counsel of the ungodly, nor standeth in the way of sinners, nor sitteth in the seat of the scornful. But his delight is in the law of the LORD; and in his law doth he meditate day and night.   *Psalms 1:1-2*

All the paths of the LORD are mercy and truth unto such as keep his covenant and his testimonies. Let integrity and uprightness preserve me; for I wait on thee.   *Psalms 25:10, 21*

But as for me, I will walk in mine integrity: redeem me, and be merciful unto me.
          Psalms 26:11

But made himself of no reputation, and took upon him the form of a servant, and was made in the likeness of men: And being found in fashion as a man, he humbled himself, and became obedient unto death, even the death of the cross.
          Philippians 2:7-8

He that handleth a matter wisely shall find good: and whoso trusteth in the LORD, happy is he.
          Proverbs 16:20

YOU WILL BE REMEMBERED FOR THE PAIN OR THE PLEASURE YOU HAVE CREATED.

RESPONSIBILITY

Let us hear the conclusion of the whole matter:
Fear God, and keep his commandments: for this is
the whole duty of man.   *Ecclesiastes 12:13*

Ye are the salt of the earth: but if the salt have lost
his savour, wherewith shall it be salted? it is thence-
forth good for nothing, but to be cast out, and to be
trodden under foot of men. Ye are the light of the
world. A city that is set on an hill cannot be hid.
Neither do men light a candle, and put it under a
bushel, but on a candlestick; and it giveth light unto
all that are in the house. Let your light so shine
before men, that they may see your good works, and
glorify your Father which is in heaven. Whosoever
therefore shall break one of these least commandments, and shall teach men so, he shall be called the
least in the kingdom of heaven: but whosoever shall
do and teach them, the same shall be called great in
the kingdom of heaven.   *Matthew 5:13-16, 19*

Then said Jesus unto his disciples, If any man will
come after me, let him deny himself, and take up his
cross, and follow me. For whosoever will save his
life shall lose it: and whosoever will lose his life for
my sake shall find it.   *Matthew 16:24-25*

**WHEN YOU DO WHAT YOU CAN, GOD WILL
DO WHAT YOU CAN'T.**

REST

And on the seventh day God ended his work which he had made; and he rested on the seventh day from all his work which he had made.

Genesis 2:2

Therefore my heart is glad, and my glory rejoiceth: my flesh also shall rest in hope.

Psalms 16:9

For with stammering lips and another tongue will he speak to this people. To whom he said, This is the rest wherewith ye may cause the weary to rest; and this is the refreshing: yet they would not hear.

Isaiah 28:11-12

Come unto me, all ye that labour and are heavy laden, and I will give you rest.   *Matthew 11:28*

To every thing there is a season, and a time to every purpose under the heaven: A time to love, and a time to hate; a time of war, and a time of peace.

Ecclesiastes 3:1, 8

Take my yoke upon you, and learn of me; for I am meek and lowly in heart: and ye shall find rest unto your souls. For my yoke is easy, and my burden is light.   *Matthew 11:29-30*

WHEN FATIGUE WALKS IN FAITH WALKS OUT. TIRED EYES RARELY SEE A GOOD FUTURE.

RICHES

Praise ye the LORD. Blessed is the man that feareth the LORD, that delighteth greatly in his commandments. His seed shall be mighty upon earth: the generation of the upright shall be blessed. Wealth and riches shall be in his house: and his righteousness endureth for ever.

Psalms 112:1-3

Happy is the man that findeth wisdom, and the man that getteth understanding. Length of days is in her right hand; and in her left hand riches and honour. *Proverbs 3:13, 16*

The wealth of the sinner is laid up for the just.
Proverbs 13:22b

Lay not up for yourselves treasures upon earth, where moth and rust doth corrupt, and where thieves break through and steal: But lay up for yourselves treasures in heaven, where neither moth nor rust doth corrupt, and where thieves do not break through nor steal: *Matthew 6:19-20*

But thou shalt remember the LORD thy God: for it is he that giveth thee power to get wealth, that he may establish his covenant which he sware unto thy fathers, as it is this day. *Deuteronomy 8:18*

SOME STUDY THE EXIT OF EVERY PENNY, OTHERS STUDY THE ENTRY OF EVERY DOLLAR. THE WISE DO BOTH.

SALVATION

All we like sheep have gone astray; we have turned every one to his own way; and the LORD hath laid on him the iniquity of us all.

Isaiah 53:6

But as many as received him, to them gave he power to become the sons of God, even to them that believe on his name: *John 1:12*

Him that cometh to me I will in no wise cast out.

John 6:37b

And they said, Believe on the Lord Jesus Christ, and thou shalt be saved, and thy house.

Acts 16:31

For all have sinned, and come short of the glory of God; *Romans 3:23*

That if thou shalt confess with thy mouth the Lord Jesus, and shalt believe in thine heart that God hath raised him from the dead, thou shalt be saved. For with the heart man believeth unto righteousness; and with the mouth confession is made unto salvation.

Romans 10:9-10

GOD NEVER CONSULTS YOUR PAST TO DETERMINE YOUR FUTURE.

SCHEDULE

Commit thy way unto the LORD; trust also in him; and he shall bring it to pass.   *Psalms 37:5*

And let the beauty of the LORD our God be upon us: and establish thou the work of our hands upon us; yea, the work of our hands establish thou it.
Psalms 90:17

To every thing there is a season, and a time to every purpose under the heaven: A time to kill, and a time to heal; a time to break down, and a time to build up;   *Ecclesiastes 3:1, 3*

And let us not be weary in well doing: for in due season we shall reap, if we faint not.
Galatians 6:9

Redeeming the time, because the days are evil.
Ephesians 5:16

And thine ears shall hear a word behind thee, saying, This is the way, walk ye in it, when ye turn to the right hand, and when ye turn to the left.
Isaiah 30:21

For the vision is yet for an appointed time, but at the end it shall speak, and not lie: though it tarry, wait for it; because it will surely come, it will not tarry.   Habakkuk 2:3

THOSE WHO DO NOT RESPECT YOUR TIME WILL NOT RESPECT YOUR WISDOM EITHER.

SEED–FAITH

While the earth remaineth, seedtime and harvest, and cold and heat, and summer and winter, and day and night shall not cease.   *Genesis 8:22*

Vow, and pay unto the LORD your God: let all that be round about him bring presents unto him that ought to be feared.   *Psalms 76:11*

Honour the LORD with thy substance, and with the firstfruits of all thine increase: So shall thy barns be filled with plenty, and thy presses shall burst out with new wine.   *Proverbs 3:9, 10*

Cast thy bread upon the waters: for thou shalt find it after many days. In the morning sow thy seed, and in the evening withhold not thine hand: for thou knowest not whether shall prosper, either this or that, or whether they both shall be alike good.
                    Ecclesiastes 11:1, 6

But this I say, He which soweth sparingly shall reap also sparingly; and he which soweth bountifully shall reap also bountifully.   *II Corinthians 9:6*

Give, and it shall be given unto you; good measure, pressed down, and shaken together, and running over, shall men give into your bosom. For with the same measure that ye mete withal it shall be measured to you again.   *Luke 6:38*

SEED FAITH IS SOWING WHAT YOU HAVE BEEN GIVEN TO CREATE WHAT YOU BEEN PROMISED.

SELF-CONFIDENCE

The LORD is my light and my salvation; whom shall I fear? the LORD is the strength of my life; of whom shall I be afraid?   *Psalms 27:1*

It is better to trust in the LORD than to put confidence in man.   *Psalms 118:8*

For the LORD shall be thy confidence, and shall keep thy foot from being taken.   *Proverbs 3:26*

Behold, I have graven thee upon the palms of my hands;   *Isaiah 49:16*

Ye have not chosen me, but I have chosen you,
                    John 15:16a

Being confident of this very thing, that he which hath begun a good work in you will perform it until the day of Jesus Christ: *Philippians 1:6*

Ye are of God, little children, and have overcome them: because greater is he that is in you, than he that is in the world.   *I John 4:4*

I can do all things through Christ which strengtheneth me.   *Philippians 4:13*

SOMEBODY HAS BEEN WAITING FOR YOU FOR A LIFETIME.

SEX

He that covereth his sins shall not prosper: but whoso confesseth and forsaketh them shall have mercy.   *Proverbs 28:13*

Flee fornication. Every sin that a man doeth is without the body; but he that committeth fornication sinneth against his own body.   *I Corinthians 6:18*

What? know ye not that your body is the temple of the Holy Ghost which is in you, which ye have of God, and ye are not your own? Therefore glorify God in your body, and in your spirit, which are God's.   *I Corinthians 6:19, 20b*

Nevertheless, to avoid fornication, let every man have his own wife, and let every woman have her own husband.   *I Corinthians 7:2*

There hath no temptation taken you but such as is common to man: but God is faithful, who will not suffer you to be tempted above that ye are able; but will with the temptation also make a way to escape, that ye may be able to bear it.
                        I Corinthians 10:13

POWER IS THE ABILITY TO WALK AWAY FROM SOMETHING YOU DESIRE TO PROTECT SOMETHING YOU LOVE.

SIN

Remember not the sins of my youth, nor my transgressions: according to thy mercy remember thou me for thy goodness' sake, O LORD.

Psalms 25:7

Hide thy face from my sins, and blot out all mine iniquities.

Psalms 51:9

If I regard iniquity in my heart, the Lord will not hear me:

Psalms 66:18

Who forgiveth all thine iniquities; who healeth all thy diseases;

Psalms 103:3

With my whole heart have I sought thee: O let me not wander from thy commandments. Thy word have I hid in mine heart, that I might not sin against thee.

Psalms 119:10-11

He that covereth his sins shall not prosper: but whoso confesseth and forsaketh them shall have mercy.

Proverbs 28:13

For all have sinned, and come short of the glory of God;

Romans 3:23

WHAT YOU FAIL TO DESTROY IN YOUR LIFE WILL EVENTUALLY DESTROY YOU.

SOUL WINNING

The fruit of the righteous is a tree of life; and he that winneth souls is wise.   *Proverbs 11:30*

Then saith he unto his disciples, The harvest truly is plenteous, but the labourers are few;
Matthew 9:37

He that is not with me is against me; and he that gathereth not with me scattereth abroad.
Matthew 12:30

And he said unto them, Go ye into all the world, and preach the gospel to every creature. He that believeth and is baptized shall be saved; but he that believeth not shall be damned.
Mark 16:15-16

Jesus answered and said unto him, Verily, verily, I say unto thee, Except a man be born again, he cannot see the kingdom of God.   *John 3:3*

Say not ye, There are yet four months, and then cometh harvest? behold, I say unto you, Lift up your eyes, and look on the fields; for they are white already to harvest.   *John 4:35*

THE BROKEN BECOME MASTERS AT MENDING.

STRESS

The LORD also will be a refuge for the oppressed, a refuge in times of trouble.

Psalms 9:9

My flesh and my heart faileth: but God is the strength of my heart, and my portion for ever.

Psalms 73:26

A thousand shall fall at thy side, and ten thousand at thy right hand; but it shall not come nigh thee. There shall no evil befall thee, neither shall any plague come nigh thy dwelling.

Psalms 91:7, 10

It is vain for you to rise up early, to sit up late, to eat the bread of sorrows: for so he giveth his beloved sleep. *Psalms 127:2*

Casting all your care upon him; for he careth for you. *I Peter 5:7*

Peace I leave with you, my peace I give unto you: not as the world giveth, give I unto you. Let not your heart be troubled, neither let it be afraid.

John 14:27

What time I am afraid, I will trust in thee.

Psalms 56:3

NEVER COMPLAIN ABOUT WHAT YOU PERMIT.

SUCCESS

And he said unto me, The LORD, before whom I walk, will send his angel with thee, and prosper thy way;   *Genesis 24:40a*

Keep therefore the words of this covenant, and do them, that ye may prosper in all that ye do.
                                        Deuteronomy 29:9

Only be thou strong and very courageous, that thou mayest observe to do according to all the law, which Moses my servant commanded thee: turn not from it to the right hand or to the left, that thou mayest prosper whithersoever thou goest. This book of the law shall not depart out of thy mouth; but thou shalt meditate therein day and night, that thou mayest observe to do according to all that is written therein: for then thou shalt make thy way prosperous, and then thou shalt have good success.
                                        Joshua 1:7-8

Pray for the peace of Jerusalem: they shall prosper that love thee.   *Psalms 122:6*

Honour the LORD with thy substance, and with the firstfruits of all thine increase: So shall thy barns be filled with plenty, and thy presses shall burst out with new wine.   *Proverbs 3:9-10*

YOUR SUCCESS IS DETERMINED BY THE PROBLEMS YOU SOLVE FOR OTHERS.

SUICIDAL THOUGHTS

Thou shalt not kill. *Exodus 20:13*

The LORD is my light and my salvation; whom shall I fear? the LORD is the strength of my life; of whom shall I be afraid? Though an host should encamp against me, my heart shall not fear: though war should rise against me, in this will I be confident. For in the time of trouble he shall hide me in his pavilion: in the secret of his tabernacle shall he hide me; he shall set me up upon a rock.
Psalms 27:1, 3, 5

Thy word have I hid in mine heart, that I might not sin against thee. *Psalms 119:11*

I will praise thee; for I am fearfully and wonderfully made: marvellous are thy works; and that my soul knoweth right well. *Psalms 139:14*

Being confident of this very thing, that he which hath begun a good work in you will perform it until the day of Jesus Christ: *Philippians 1:6*

Weeping may endure for a night, but joy cometh in the morning. Psalms 30:5b

YOUR FOCUS DETERMINES WHAT YOU FEEL. WHEN YOU CHANGE YOUR FOCUS YOU CHANGE YOUR FEELINGS.

TEAMWORK

Behold, how good and how pleasant it is for brethren to dwell together in unity!

Psalms 133:1

Two are better than one; because they have a good reward for their labour. For if they fall, the one will lift up his fellow: but woe to him that is alone when he falleth; for he hath not another to help him up. And if one prevail against him, two shall withstand him; and a threefold cord is not quickly broken.

Ecclesiastes 4:9-10, 12

Can two walk together, except they be agreed?

Amos 3:3

Again I say unto you, That if two of you shall agree on earth as touching any thing that they shall ask, it shall be done for them of my Father which is in heaven.

Matthew 18:19

And when the day of Pentecost was fully come, they were all with one accord in one place.

Acts 2:1

Knowing that whatsoever good thing any man doeth, the same shall he receive of the Lord, whether he be bond or free.

Ephesians 6:8

WHAT YOU MAKE HAPPEN FOR OTHERS, GOD WILL MAKE HAPPEN FOR YOU.

TEMPTATION

Thy word have I hid in mine heart, that I might not sin against thee.   *Psalms 119:11*

There hath no temptation taken you but such as is common to man: but God is faithful, who will not suffer you to be tempted above that ye are able; but will with the temptation also make a way to escape, that ye may be able to bear it.
I Corinthians 10:13

Put on the whole armour of God, that ye may be able to stand against the wiles of the devil. Above all, taking the shield of faith, wherewith ye shall be able to quench all the fiery darts of the wicked.
Ephesians 6:11, 16

Submit yourselves therefore to God. Resist the devil, and he will flee from you.   *James 4:7*

The Lord knoweth how to deliver the godly out of temptations,   *II Peter 2:9a*

When the enemy shall come in like a flood, the Spirit of the LORD shall lift up a standard against him.   *Isaiah 59:19b*

WHAT YOU'RE WILLING TO WALK AWAY FROM DETERMINES WHAT GOD WILL BRING TO YOU.

TEN COMMANDMENTS

Thou shalt have no other gods before me. Thou shalt not make unto thee any graven image, or any likeness of any thing that is in heaven above, or that is in the earth beneath, or that is in the water under the earth: Thou shalt not bow down thyself to them, nor serve them: for I the LORD thy God am a jealous God, Thou shalt not take the name of the LORD thy God in vain; for the LORD will not hold him guiltless that taketh his name in vain. Remember the sabbath day, to keep it holy. Six days shalt thou labour, and do all thy work: But the seventh day is the sabbath of the LORD thy God: Honour thy father and thy mother: that thy days may be long upon the land which the LORD thy God giveth thee. Thou shalt not kill. Thou shalt not commit adultery. Thou shalt not steal. Thou shalt not bear false witness against thy neighbour. Thou shalt not covet.

Exodus 20:3-11a,12-17a

Thou knowest the commandments, Do not commit adultery, Do not kill, Do not steal, Do not bear false witness, Defraud not, Honour thy father and mother. And he answered and said unto him, Master, all these have I observed from my youth.

Mark 10:19-20

YOUR FUTURE IS DETERMINED BY YOUR ABILITY TO FOLLOW INSTRUCTIONS.

THOUGHTS

Many, O LORD my God, are thy wonderful works which thou hast done, and thy thoughts which are to us-ward: they cannot be reckoned up in order unto thee: if I would declare and speak of them, they are more than can be numbered.   *Psalms 40:5*

The thoughts of the righteous are right: but the counsels of the wicked are deceit.
Proverbs 12:5

Commit thy works unto the LORD, and thy thoughts shall be established.   *Proverbs 16:3*

For as he thinketh in his heart, so is he:
Proverbs 23:7a

For I know the thoughts that I think toward you, saith the LORD, thoughts of peace, and not of evil, to give you an expected end.   *Jeremiah 29:11*

Finally, brethren, whatsoever things are true, whatsoever things are honest, whatsoever things are just, whatsoever things are pure, whatsoever things are lovely, whatsoever things are of good report; if there be any virtue, and if there be any praise, think on these things.   *Philippians 4:8*

LOSERS FOCUS ON WHAT THEY ARE GOING THROUGH WHILE CHAMPIONS FOCUS ON WHAT THEY ARE GOING TO.

TITHING

Thou shalt truly tithe all the increase of thy seed, that the field bringeth forth year by year.

Deuteronomy 14:22

Honour the LORD with thy substance, and with the firstfruits of all thine increase: So shall thy barns be filled with plenty, and thy presses shall burst out with new wine.   *Proverbs 3:9-10*

Bring ye all the tithes into the storehouse, that there may be meat in mine house, and prove me now herewith, saith the LORD of hosts, if I will not open you the windows of heaven, and pour you out a blessing, that there shall not be room enough to receive it. And I will rebuke the devourer for your sakes, and he shall not destroy the fruits of your ground; neither shall your vine cast her fruit before the time in the field, saith the LORD of hosts.

Malachi 3:10-11

Woe unto you, scribes and Pharisees, hypocrites! for ye pay tithe of mint and anise and cummin, and have omitted the weightier matters of the law, judgment, mercy, and faith: these ought ye to have done, and not to leave the other undone.

Matthew 23:23

WHEN YOU LET GO OF WHAT IS IN YOUR HAND GOD WILL LET GO OF WHAT'S IN HIS HAND. TITHE IS A MEASURE OF YOUR OBEDIENCE, AN OFFERING IS A MEASURE OF YOUR GENEROSITY.

TRUTH

All the paths of the LORD are mercy and truth unto such as keep his covenant and his testimonies.
Psalms 25:10

Jesus saith unto him, I am the way, the truth, and the life: no man cometh unto the Father, but by me.
John 14:6

Finally, brethren, whatsoever things are true, whatsoever things are honest, whatsoever things are just, whatsoever things are pure, whatsoever things are lovely, whatsoever things are of good report; if there be any virtue, and if there be any praise, think on these things.   *Philippians 4:8*

Seeing ye have purified your souls in obeying the truth through the Spirit unto unfeigned love of the brethren, see that ye love one another with a pure heart fervently: *I Peter 1:22*

God is not a man, that he should lie; neither the son of man, that he should repent: hath he said, and shall he not do it? or hath he spoken, and shall he not make it good?   *Numbers 23:19*

TRUTH IS THE MOST POWERFUL THING ON EARTH BECAUSE IT IS THE ONLY THING THAT CANNOT BE CHANGED.

UNEMPLOYMENT

Trust in the LORD, and do good; so shalt thou dwell in the land, and verily thou shalt be fed.
Psalms 37:3

Behold, I will do a new thing; now it shall spring forth; shall ye not know it? I will even make a way in the wilderness, and rivers in the desert.
Isaiah 43:19

For even when we were with you, this we commanded you, that if any would not work, neither should he eat.
II Thessalonians 3:10

Love not sleep, lest thou come to poverty; open thine eyes, and thou shalt be satisfied with bread.
Proverbs 20:13

Whatsoever thy hand findeth to do, do it with thy might;
Ecclesiastes 9:10a

For verily I say unto you, That whosoever shall say unto this mountain, Be thou removed, and be thou cast into the sea; and shall not doubt in his heart, but shall believe that those things which he saith shall come to pass; he shall have whatsoever he saith.
Mark 11:23

GO WHERE YOU'RE CELEBRATED, NOT WHERE YOU'RE TOLERATED.

VICTORY

Then sang Moses and the children of Israel this song unto the LORD, and spake, saying, I will sing unto the LORD, for he hath triumphed gloriously: the horse and his rider hath he thrown into the sea.
Exodus 15:1

O my God, I trust in thee: let me not be ashamed, let not mine enemies triumph over me.
Psalms 25:2

For thou, LORD, hast made me glad through thy work: I will triumph in the works of thy hands.
Psalms 92:4

Save us, O LORD our God, and gather us from among the heathen, to give thanks unto thy holy name, and to triumph in thy praise.
Psalms 106:47

And they overcame him by the blood of the Lamb, and by the word of their testimony; and they loved not their lives unto the death.
Revelation 12:11

I can do all things through Christ which strengtheneth me.
Philippians 4:13

YOU WILL NEVER REACH THE PALACE TALKING LIKE A PEASANT.

VISION

In a dream, in a vision of the night, when deep sleep falleth upon men, in slumberings upon the bed; Then he openeth the ears of men, and sealeth their instruction, That he may withdraw man from his purpose, and hide pride from man.

Job 33:15-17

Where there is no vision, the people perish: but he that keepeth the law, happy is he.

Proverbs 29:18

Write the vision, and make it plain upon tables, that he may run that readeth it. For the vision is yet for an appointed time, but at the end it shall speak, and not lie: though it tarry, wait for it; because it will surely come, it will not tarry. *Habakkuk 2:2a, 3*

Enlarge the place of thy tent, and let them stretch forth the curtains of thine habitations: spare not, lengthen thy cords, and strengthen thy stakes;

Isaiah 54:2

And it shall come to pass afterward, that I will pour out my spirit upon all flesh; and your sons and your daughters shall prophesy, your old men shall dream dreams, your young men shall see visions:

Joel 2:28

STOP LOOKING AT WHERE YOU HAVE BEEN AND START LOOKING AT WHERE YOU CAN BE.

Vows

When thou shalt vow a vow unto the LORD thy God, thou shalt not slack to pay it: for the LORD thy God will surely require it of thee; and it would be sin in thee.   *Deuteronomy 23:21*

If a man vow a vow unto the LORD, or swear an oath to bind his soul with a bond; he shall not break his word, he shall do according to all that proceedeth out of his mouth.   *Numbers 30:2*

Vow, and pay unto the LORD your God: let all that be round about him bring presents unto him that ought to be feared.   *Psalms 76:11*

He that hath pity upon the poor lendeth unto the LORD; and that which he hath given will he pay him again.   *Proverbs 19:17*

Better is it that thou shouldest not vow, than that thou shouldest vow and not pay.

Ecclesiastes 5:5

And Paul after this tarried there yet a good while, and then took his leave of the brethren, and sailed thence into Syria, and with him Priscilla and Aquila; having shorn his head in Cenchrea: for he had a vow.   *Acts 18:18*

THE WAVES OF YESTERDAY'S BROKEN VOWS WILL SPLASH ON THE SHORES OF TOMORROW.

WEALTH

But thou shalt remember the LORD thy God: for it is he that giveth thee power to get wealth, that he may establish his covenant which he sware unto thy fathers, as it is this day.   *Deuteronomy 8:18*

Praise ye the LORD. Blessed is the man that feareth the LORD, that delighteth greatly in his commandments. His seed shall be mighty upon earth: the generation of the upright shall be blessed. Wealth and riches shall be in his house: and his righteousness endureth for ever.

Psalms 112:1-3

The wealth of the sinner is laid up for the just.

Proverbs 13:22b

Charge them that are rich in this world, that they be not highminded, nor trust in uncertain riches, but in the living God, who giveth us richly all things to enjoy; That they do good, that they be rich in good works, ready to distribute, willing to communicate; Laying up in store for themselves a good foundation against the time to come, that they may lay hold on eternal life.   *I Timothy 6:17-19*

And he said unto them, Take heed, and beware of covetousness: for a man's life consisteth not in the abundance of the things which he possesseth.

Luke 12:15

WEALTH IS WHEN YOU HAVE A LOT OF SOMETHING YOU LOVE.

WINNING

Then sang Moses and the children of Israel this song unto the LORD, and spake, saying, I will sing unto the LORD, for he hath triumphed gloriously: the horse and his rider hath he thrown into the sea.
Exodus 15:1

For thou, LORD, hast made me glad through thy work: I will triumph in the works of thy hands.
Psalms 92:4

The fruit of the righteous is a tree of life; and he that winneth souls is wise.   *Proverbs 11:30*

For I will give you a mouth and wisdom, which all your adversaries shall not be able to gainsay nor resist.   *Luke 21:15*

Ye are of God, little children, and have overcome them: because greater is he that is in you, than he that is in the world.   *I John 4:4*

And such as do wickedly against the covenant shall he corrupt by flatteries: but the people that do know their God shall be strong, and do exploits.
Daniel 11:32

Then he answered and spake unto me, saying, This is the word of the LORD unto Zerubbabel, saying, Not by might, nor by power, but by my spirit, saith the LORD of hosts.   *Zechariah 4:6*

YOU WILL NEVER OUTGROW WARFARE. YOU SIMPLY MUST LEARN TO FIGHT.

WISDOM

Wisdom and knowledge is granted unto thee; and I will give thee riches, and wealth, and honour, such as none of the kings have had that have been before thee, neither shall there any after thee have the like.
II Chronicles 1:12

The fear of the LORD is the beginning of wisdom: a good understanding have all they that do his commandments: his praise endureth for ever.
Psalms 111:10

Wisdom is the principal thing; therefore get wisdom: and with all thy getting get understanding.
Proverbs 4:7

Exalt her, and she shall promote thee: she shall bring thee to honour, when thou dost embrace her.
Proverbs 4:8

If any of you lack wisdom, let him ask of God, that giveth to all men liberally, and upbraideth not; and it shall be given him.
James 1:5

Happy is the man that findeth wisdom, and the man that getteth understanding.
Proverbs 3:13

WISDOM IS THE ONLY REAL NEED YOU WILL EVER HAVE.

WORK

Six days shall work be done, but on the seventh day there shall be to you an holy day, a sabbath of rest to the LORD: *Exodus 35:2a*

That the LORD thy God may bless thee in all the work of thine hands. *Deuteronomy 24:19b*

Be strong, all ye people of the land, saith the LORD, and work: for I am with you, saith the LORD of hosts: *Haggai 2:4b*

And having food and raiment let us be therewith content. *I Timothy 6:8*

For the people had a mind to work. *Nehemiah 4:6b*

For the workman is worthy of his meat. *Matthew 10:10b*

Six days shalt thou labour, and do all thy work: *Exodus 20:9*

Moreover it is required in stewards, that a man be found faithful. *I Corinthians 4:2*

Seest thou a man diligent in his business? He shall stand before kings; he shall not stand before mean men. *Proverbs 22:29*

MONEY IS MERELY A REWARD FOR SOLVING PROBLEMS.

99

WORRY

And thou shalt be secure, because there is hope; yea, thou shalt dig about thee, and thou shalt take thy rest in safety.   *Job 11:18*

Fret not thyself because of evil men, neither be thou envious at the wicked;   *Proverbs 24:19*

In righteousness shalt thou be established: thou shalt be far from oppression; for thou shalt not fear: and from terror; for it shall not come near thee.
                                            Isaiah 54:14

Be careful for nothing; but in every thing by prayer and supplication with thanksgiving let your requests be made known unto God. And the peace of God, which passeth all understanding, shall keep your hearts and minds through Christ Jesus. Finally, brethren, whatsoever things are true, whatsoever things are honest, whatsoever things are just, whatsoever things are pure, whatsoever things are lovely, whatsoever things are of good report; if there be any virtue, and if there be any praise, think on these things.   *Philippians 4:6-8*

Are not two sparrows sold for a farthing? and one of them shall not fall on the ground without your Father. But the very hairs of your head are all numbered. Fear ye not therefore, ye are of more value than many sparrows.   *Matthew 10:31*

NOTHING IS EVER AS BAD AS IT FIRST APPEARS.

WORSHIP

Give unto the LORD the glory due unto his name:
bring an offering, and come before him: worship the
LORD in the beauty of holiness.
I Chronicles 16:29

It is a good thing to give thanks unto the LORD,
and to sing praises unto thy name, O most High: To
show forth thy lovingkindness in the morning, and
thy faithfulness every night,   *Psalms 92:1-2*

Now we know that God heareth not sinners: but if
any man be a worshipper of God, and doeth his will,
him he heareth.   *John 9:31*

I will extol thee, my God, O king; and I will bless
thy name for ever and ever. Every day will I bless
thee; and I will praise thy name for ever and ever.
Great is the LORD, and greatly to be praised; and
his greatness is unsearchable.   *Psalms 145:1-3*

And Jesus answered and said unto him, Get thee
behind me, Satan: for it is written, Thou shalt worship the Lord thy God, and him only shalt thou serve.
Luke 4:8

**TRUE WORSHIP IS NOT FORCED PASSION. IT'S
AN UNAVOIDABLE INTIMACY. IT'S THE LOVE-
ROOM WHERE YOUR FUTURE IS BORN.**

MAY I INVITE YOU TO MAKE JESUS CHRIST THE LORD OF YOUR LIFE?

The Bible says, "That if thou shalt confess with thy mouth the Lord Jesus, and shalt believe in thine heart that God hath raised him from the dead, thou shalt be saved. For with the heart man believeth unto righteousness; and with the mouth confession is made unto salvation" (Romans 10:9-10).

To receive Jesus Christ as Lord and Savior of your life, please pray this prayer from your heart today!

"Dear Jesus, I believe that You died for me and rose again on the third day. I confess to You that I am a sinner. I need Your love and forgiveness. Come into my life, forgive my sins, and give me eternal life. I confess You now as my Lord. Thank You for my salvation! I walk in Your peace and joy from this day forward. Amen."

Signed _____

Date _____

Return this today!

☐ Yes, Mike! I made a decision to accept Christ as my personal Savior today. Please send me my free gift of your book *31 Keys to a New Beginning* to help me with my new life in Christ.

Name _____

Address _____
(Please Print)

City _____ State _____ Zip _____

Phone (___) _____

Mail to:
Dr. Mike Murdock   P.O. Box 99   Dallas, Texas 75221

ORDER OTHER VERSIONS OF THE

ONE-MINUTE POCKET BIBLE

FOR FATHERS, FOR MOTHERS, FOR TEENAGERS, FOR ACHIEVERS

$7.00 EACH

Mail To: Mike Murdock
The Wisdom Center P.O. Box 99 Dallas, TX 75221

Mike, please send me The One-Minute
Pocket Bible(s) for: _____

_____

_____

Name _____

Address_____

City_____State_____

Zip _____

Phone _____

❑ Check   ❑ Money Order   ❑ Cash

❑ Visa   ❑ Mastercard   ❑ Amex

Card# _____

Expiration Date: _____

Signature: _____

ABOUT MIKE MURDOCK

▶ Began full-time evangelism at the age of 19, which has continued for 28 years.

▶ Has traveled and spoken to more than 11,000 audiences in 36 countries, including East Africa, the Orient, and Europe.

▶ Noted author of 57 books, including the best sellers, Wisdom for Winning, Dream-Seeds, and The Double Diamond Principle.

▶ Has composed more than 1,200 songs such as I Am Blessed, You Can Make It, Jesus Just The Mention of Your Name, recorded by many gospel artists.

▶ Is the Founder of the Wisdom Training Center, for the training of those entering the ministry.

▶ Has a weekly television program called Wisdom for Crisis Times.

4 POWER-PACKED TAPE SERIES BY MIKE MURDOCK

HOW TO WALK THROUGH FIRE

The 4 basic causes of conflict and how to react in a personal crisis, which are extremely helpful for those who are walking through the fires of marriage difficulty, divorce, depression and financial adversity.
(TS5) Six Tape Series

$30

THE ASSIGNMENT

Do you wonder why you are here? What are you to do? These tapes will unlock the hidden treasures inside you to fulfill the Assignment God has called you to. 160 Wisdom Keys that can reveal the purpose of God.
(TS22) Six Tape Series

$30

**WOMEN
THAT MEN
CANNOT
FORGET**

D iscover the success secrets of two of the most remarkable women in history...and how their secrets can help you achieve your goals! Both men and women will enjoy these wisdom secrets from the lives of Ruth and Esther. (TS31) Six Tape Series

$30

**THE
RASSHOPPER
COMPLEX**

A must for those who need more self-confidence! It reveals the secrets of overcoming every giant you face in achieving your personal dreams and goals. (TS3) Six Tape Series

$30

**Order All Four Series
& Pay Only $100**

6 Wisdom Books

WISDOM FOR CRISIS TIMES

Discover the Wisdom Keys to Dealing with tragedies, stress and times of crisis, secrets that will unlock the questions the right way to react in life situations. (Paperback) (BK08) 118 Pages.....$7

SEEDS OF WISDOM

One-Year Daily Devotional. A 374 page devotional with topics on dreams and goals, relationships, miracles, prosperity and more! (Paperback) (BK02) 374 Pages.....$10

ONE-YEAR TOPICAL BIBLE

A One-Minute refer-
ence Bible. 365 topics;
spiritual, topical and
easy to read. A col-
lection of Scriptures
relating to specific
topics that challenge and
concern you.
(Paperback)
(BK03) 374 Pages.....$10

THE DOUBLE DIAMOND PRINCIPLE

58 Master Secrets For
Total Success, in the
life of Jesus that will
help you achieve your
dreams and goals.
(Paperback)
(BK71) 118 Pages.....$7

WISDOM FOR WINNING

The best-selling handbook for achieving success. If you desire to be successful and happy, this is the book for you! (Paperback)
(BK23) 280 Pages.....$9

DREAM SEEDS

What do you dream of doing with your life? What would you attempt to do if you knew it was impossible to fail? This 118-page book helps you answer these questions and much more! (Paperback)
(BK02) 374 Pages.....$10

ORDER FORM

ITEM NO.	NAME OF ITEM	QTY.	PRICE PER ITEM	TOTAL
#TS22	The Assignment Tapes		30.00	$
#TS5	How To Walk Through Fire Tapes		30.00	$
#TS3	The Grasshopper Complex Tapes		30.00	$
#TS3	Women Men Cannot Forget Tapes		30.00	$
	All 4 Tape Series for $100.00			$
#B11	Dream Seeds Book		8.00	$
#B1	Wisdom For Winning Book		10.00	$
#B25	Seeds of Wisdom Book (374 pgs)		10.00	$
#B39	Double Diamond Principle Book		8.00	$
#B40	Wisdom For Crisis Times Book		8.00	$
#B31	One Minute Topical Bible (374 pgs)		10.00	$
#B50	One Minute Pocket Bible For Achievers		5.00	$
#B51	One Minute Pocket Bible For Fathers		5.00	$
#B52	One Minute Pocket Bible For Mothers		5.00	$
#B53	One Minute Pocket Bible for Teenagers		5.00	$
SORRY NO C.O.D.'s	Add 10% For Shipping			$
	(Canada add 20%)			$
	Enclosed is my Seed-Faith Gift for Your Ministry.			$
#DC10	Total Amount Enclosed			$

Please Print

Name

Address

City

State _____ * Zip

Phone (hm) _____ (wk)

☐ Check ☐ Money Order ☐ Cash ☐ Visa ☐ MasterCard ☐ AMEX

Card#

Signature _____ Exp. Date _____

☐ Send Free Catalog & Free Subsription To Newsletter *Wisdom Talk*

Mail To: MIKE MURDOCK • P.O. Box 99 • Dallas, Texas 75221